MIRACLE IN THE DARK

*The untold truth about
near-death experiences
and the afterlife*

John Dudley Aldworth

Author of acclaimed 'Forbidden History' and 'Noah's Land'

Copyright © 2023 John Dudley Aldworth

First edition published January 2023.

The moral right of the author to full ownership of the copyright of Miracle in the Dark' has been asserted. All rights are reserved. The book may not be reproduced in part or whole without prior written permission from the publisher. However, extracts for the purpose of Bible study, sermons, and reviews in magazines, newspapers, radio and television, and quotations in other books are allowed.

Publisher: **Truthful History Publications**
Email: john.aldworth@hotmail.com

Cover Design by: Colleen Kaluza

Prepared for publication by: WordWyze Publishing Ltd
            http://wordwyze.nz

Most Scriptures are from the Authorised King James Version, Public Domain.

Scripture quotations marked (AMP) taken from the Amplified Bible (AMP), Copyright © 2015 by The Lockman Foundation. Used by permission, www.lockman.org.

Scripture quotations marked (NIV) taken from The Holy Bible, New International Version® (NIV®) Copyright© 1973, 1978, 1984, 2011 by Biblica, Inc.® Used by permission. www.biblica.com.

Scripture references marked (NKJV) are from the New King James Version. Copyright © 1982 by Thomas Nelson, Inc. Used by permission. All rights reserved.

A catalogue record for this book is available from the National Library of New Zealand.

Paperback ISBN: 978-0-473-67235-5
E-pub ISBN: 978-0-473-67236-2

How to Buy this Book:

Copies of 'Miracle in the Dark' and John's other books, are available in New Zealand direct from the author, but are also available from international online book distributors including Amazon and Mighty Ape, and can be ordered through your local library.

John Dudley Aldworth - Email: john.aldworth@hotmail.com

Contents

JOURNEY TO THE AFTERLIFE

Outside, it was day, but down in the cave, it was night. Underground blackness is so intense that without a lamp, one forgets one has eyes in seconds. Moving in such darkness is then only by hearing and touch. As a boy of 10, I brought this plunge into the black on myself when I broke the cardinal rule of never venturing underground alone.

Failing to find a friend to accompany me, I had set off alone to photograph upper chamber calcite formations in Giant's Hole, the river cave that starts high on the Peak above Castleton in Derbyshire, England and descends nearly a thousand feet to the valley below.

My inward, downward route was along a descending stream passage, then up a 35-foot rope climb to an upper gallery rich in stalactites, stalagmites and flowing calcite formations I intended to photograph. Of course, as a lone explorer, I took precautions. My haversack carried camera, flashlight, spare cap lamp bulbs, even a candle and matches.

Problem was, I had to put the bag down to take pictures and just when I did, the bulb in my cap lamp went out for the second time. No problem, I thought; I have a spare in the bag. But now, in the dark, I could not find the haversack, despite crawling around the rock floor in widening circles, feeling for it.

Eventually, it dawned on me my best move was to try to find my way out before I lost all sense of direction. Far off, I could just hear the faint tinkle of water and thought that if I headed toward it and kept by touch to the left side 'wall' of the chamber, it would lead me to the top of the ravine above the stream bed. The gulf here was bridged by a rocky parapet which, if I could scramble over it, led to the other side where a rope allowed an easy climb down.

But such escape never happened. The 'left side rock face' I was following was blocked at one point by a huge boulder, and in feeling my way, I went round the right (and wrong) side of it, instead of continuing leftwards along the passage wall. Noise from the stream below now became very loud, and I inched forward feet first, but instead of finding the parapet, slid over the edge and fell some 35 feet down the ravine, ricocheting from one rock face to another.

My fall ended as I slammed head first into the rocky stream bed. I believe the miner's pit hat I wore saved me from instant death, but in the shock, I left my battered body and began the journey to another world that all who have had a near-death experience undergo.

My first impression was of a blackness darker than that of the cave I was in. Somehow, I was made aware that this was also a darkness in my own soul. There was a strong sense that my very limited and childish outlook on life was also my prison. Though no one spoke to me, and I heard no words as such, I was led to realise my life was incarcerated in ignorance and lack of light.

This 'dungeon' then seemed to become a tunnel that I found myself ascending. And along the way, my life was re-reeled before me. All my sins, selfishness, blunders, hurts, and dark deeds were reproduced and appeared as 'missing pieces', holes and blemishes in this incomplete but fast coming together jigsaw puzzle.

Then something wonderful happened. As the moving panorama continued, better pieces were supplied to fill holes in the picture and complete the puzzle as it unrolled. To my amazement, the many blotches, holes and blemishes in my record were replaced with good deeds that, apparently, I could have done but, in reality, had not. Frame by fast-moving frame, my badly torn tapestry of misdeeds was made whole, revealing a vista of a worthwhile, satisfying life of righteous accomplishment that stretched into the future. The only problem was, I knew this new life was not mine.

Talk about having the *'righteousness of God that is by faith'*[1]! I was seeing it rolled out before my eyes, as it were, had I in reality been able to see through them. Instead, I now believe I saw it then through another faculty, that of my spirit. More on that later. With my existence to date thus seemingly put right, I was overwhelmed by a sense that such a righteous life was my true destiny, the purpose for which I was born. And I longed with deep yearning for it to be so.

But more. I now began to see light; not ordinary light, but a light of great goodness, warmth and acceptance. It drew me closer in, much as a strong magnet irresistibly draws iron filings to itself. It was then borne in on me that in this light, there were Beings; indeed, it seemed the light itself emanated from them and that they lived within it and were it.

My attention was now focussed on these Beings, and from somewhere deep down within whoever or whatever I still was at that time, there surged up a strong and irrepressible desire to be with and remain with them forever. It was, I felt, the true home to which I belonged.

---

[1] Philippians 3:9

More than that, I realised this realm of being was limitless in scope. Stretching out into the distance, I glimpsed vistas of huge enlightening experiences, each with the prospect of vast, new and profound understanding. In impressions I could not put into words, I sensed that this is how it should be for every human being, how it was intended to be. A living of love, life and joy as one is taken on into ever-expanding and wonderfully good experiences in which one would play a part.

Teams of wild horses could not have dragged me from such bliss. I knew without doubt, this peaceful love realm was where I truly belonged. Only here could I become what I was meant to be; only here could I fulfil my destiny; only here could I truly be at 'home'. So, with all that was within me, I determined to stay and never leave.

But it was not to be. For suddenly, and gently at first, then with increasing force, I was pulled away from this Paradise of bliss, back down the dark tunnel and into my body. I knew I was back to 'normal' life on earth because of the tremendous jolt of pain with which I 'awoke', if that is the right way to describe it.

The physical reality now was that I was lying in the stream bed, water rushing over my face, struggling to breathe and finding myself paralysed and unable to move my limbs. Sharp pain came in spasms but eventually, I found myself able to move a little, then more. So, still in darkness, I began to crawl upwards, feeling my way by the water running against me.

Over an hour later, I emerged from the cave entrance into daylight. I then faced a 35-mile bike ride up hill and down dale back to my then home in Rochdale, Lancashire. To this day, I do not know how I managed it. At the time, I told nobody about this experience; indeed, it was only years later, after other spiritual experiences, that I opened up and learned that others also had been taken into what appeared to be another world, another dimension. And it's taken most of my lifetime to address the big question of what the experience really meant.

Years earlier, I had what I believe was my first NDE when in a coma and delirious in hospital. I was very young at the time and only vaguely remember being in another place, if not another time, which seemed far more real than my then surroundings. I executed a complete pass on its relevance or meaning.

Two down, one to go. My last 'other worldly' encounter was far more recent and of a very different kind. In hospital, with an extremely debilitating illness that left me sleepless, shivering and scarcely able to crawl to the toilet, I experienced 50 shades of horror. People I knew became demons cursing and plotting to destroy me.

Dark shades drew about me, and I realised I was truly circling the drain on the brink of dying. I cried out to God to save me. Thankfully, my prayers were heard, and I was delivered but it took weeks to recover. So, had I, in these near-death experiences, really encountered heaven and hell? Read on to find the answer.

Giants Hole. Entrance to the cave where the author had his near-death experience.

PREFACE

Death is inevitable but we mostly try not to think, still less talk about it. Thus, departing this life is a largely taboo subject. Few churches hand out guides on how to die or face what follows. Death's aftermath is not on most people's bucket lists. It doesn't make a popular sermon, still less an article in the local rag.

Nevertheless, most folk believe that at their earthly demise they will go to heaven. Thus, they blithely ignore the biblical warning that for those deemed undeserving of heaven, a hell awaits. Indeed, Psalm 9:17 disturbingly insists: *'The wicked shall be turned into hell and all the nations that forget God'*.

The sober fact is that each year multiple millions do die, leaving a big question mark over what happens to them after that. Yet those that return from a 'near-death experience' tell of a realm beyond this life in which there is joy inexpressible. Indeed, hardened atheists emerge from near-death, out-of-the-body experiences (NDE and OBE for short and NDEr for near-death experiencer), saying they met God and even saw Jesus. Others see Beings in dazzling light and return determined to live a better life, caring for others.

So, is there a real message from God to us in the near-death experience? And if there is, have we taken it on board? This book suggests a profound truth about being taken near-dead to an apparent 'life after life' has been missed, even though it is hiding in plain sight.

First though, we must ask: Is the near-death experience actually real? Or is it the result of chemical changes in the brain or some other material cause? Is it, as some fundamental Christians hold, a delusion from the devil giving false hope of life after death?

Come to that, are death and hell real? Does God turn his back on those who wish to enter heaven? Is there a judgement after death which we must all face? Is the ecstasy of joy, peace and acceptance that most NDErs encounter, for real or the product of a dying brain? Above all, we must decide whether there truly is life after death or is bodily demise the end of us?

In this book, I seek to persuade you that NDEs are not only true but that they also contain a message from God, one that, if heeded, can be a passport to glory and a life beyond the grave. What's more, I am convinced that NDEs teach important lessons unlearned by most people about who we really are and what we can be in the future.

So maybe near-death experiences are God's calling card for eternity to those who undergo them. Maybe they offer real hope of a life with God in future to all who accept what He is saying through them. I have written this book in the hope that that is so. Fact is, I have personally had three near-death encounters, two in my childhood and one in my later years. And for much of my life, I have pondered their enlarging and life-changing effect, before concluding their message is the vital key to the future for all who will believe it. The rest of this book seeks to explain why.

Chapter 1 -
SO WHAT DID IT MEAN?

After the cave episode, I had to ask: Did I really have an out-of-the-body experience (OBE) along with my NDE? It's an intriguing question because, unlike most NDErs, I was not in any sort of light to begin with. You see, most near-death experiences take place in daylight or well-lit hospital rooms. But in the cave I was exploring, darkness was absolute. There was no light at all, save that of my cap lamp which, as explained, had suddenly failed. Trying to find my way out, I fell many feet down a ravine to the rocky stream bed below.

Then began a profound near-death experience. Cave darkness may have led to the accident, but I only knew for sure I had been out of my body when, much later, I was hit by extreme pain and shock on re-entering it. As they say, I then knew I was alive because it hurt so much. Perhaps the most important lesson I learned during this strange 'out-of-body' journey to the 'other world' in a pitch-black cave, is that there is an even darker night to be found in one's own soul. But this is only one of the realisations that we come to in an NDE experience. Others are also important.

Today the out-of-body (OBE) and near-death experience (NDE) has become a much-puzzled-over phenomenon. I am only one of many who have been caught up in what all who have undergone it see as a visit, no matter how brief, to the realm of those who apparently live on after death. Actually, around 30 million people a year come back to tell of their encounters with this other world. What's more, the pages of history carry the stories of ancient men and women who tell of the same occurrences, millennia ago.

And, although a few seem to encounter horror there, most NDErs by far speak of glimpsing holy 'Beings' in white and being overcome by exquisite feelings of peace, acceptance, joy and holiness in their journey into a life beyond. Many who find themselves outside their body say, as I do, that such out-of-this-world ecstasy is more real and more delightful than anything they've known in their 'real life' before or afterwards.

Of course, it's still an open question as to what such experiences really mean. Neurologists, psychologists, other doctors and scientists have examined thousands of NDE cases and sought hard to find material, chemical or neurological reasons for them. All to no avail, it seems, because when put against the testimony of those who have actually left their bodies and returned, their theories simply cannot account for what seem inexplicable facts. For example, many OBE people report in authentic and accurate detail parts of hospitals and outdoor places they saw when out of the body but had never visited or seen prior to that in their pre-NDE life.

So, what to make of my own journey into this other world? It's been a puzzle to me for many years, and what I've come to understand about it will take the rest of this book to explain. But in short, let me say that NDE and OBE events are absolutely real. Although brain dead and/or dying, NDErs really do travel beyond their surroundings, view their bodies from above, enter a tunnel of darkness and encounter white 'Beings' who radiate peace, acceptance, joy and **ecstasy**. The latter word is important. It transliterates the Greek word *ekstasis,* which the Bible translates as 'vision' or 'trance' but which also means ecstatic happiness.

This joyful experience ended when I was suddenly returned to my body and 'came to' with a sharp jolt of pain. I lay paralysed in the stream bed for what may have been an hour before I found the strength to crawl upstream and eventually reach daylight at the cave mouth. I then faced a 35-mile cycle ride over the hills to reach my home in Rochdale. As said, somehow, I made it. All up, it amounted to a miracle, a 'miracle in the dark'.

Chapter 2 -
A PROFOUND LIFE-
CHANGING EXPERIENCE

Comparatively few undergo it and live to tell the tale; far more die and are heard from no more. Yet the NDE is a real, profound, universal and well-documented human experience. Psychologists still puzzle over it; doctors and scientists conduct detailed research into it and a plethora of theories have been advanced to describe it. However, few provide a watertight explanation of what actually occurs; still less provide a sensible reason for the phenomenon that satisfies those who have undergone it.

I have spent decades seeking a plausible understanding of what really happened to me when, as a 10-year-old boy, I tumbled down a ravine inside a deep, dark cave with a stream running through the bottom of it. As said, my cap lamp bulb failed, and when I fell, I landed on my head on rocks in the stream bed below. I believe that a 'miracle in the dark' from God may well have intervened to prevent what otherwise might have been death or permanent injury. I wore a miner's hat which rests directly on one's head despite its webbing, meaning there is only about one-sixteenth of an inch of matter protecting the skull. But by some miracle, I survived my head-first landing on the rocks.

It has been said, somewhat unkindly, that ongoing damage from this fall explains why I am who I am and why I believe in deep spiritual experiences. Now, I freely admit that I don't follow the crowd, run with the herd, nor necessarily go along with the prevailing mind set of 'church' or the society in which I live, but often think and believe 'outside the square'. If others think this strange, well, they're entitled to their opinion.

But back to my NDE. I remember the plunge down the ravine, banging off the rock walls as I fell – but then knew only blackness. (Not just the darkness of being in a cave deep underground, that is, where the absence of light is such that within seconds of being plunged into it, one forgets one has eyes and quickly learns to move by touch and sound alone, which I was already experiencing.)

No, this was another darkness, a personal night, a spiritual and emotional experience of being locked into a very small self which I was shown could, and should, have been much bigger, much better. My severely limited understanding amounted to an ignorance from which, in my NDE, I instinctively wanted to escape.

I should explain that though young, I was an aspiring potholer and had on several occasions explored the British Pennine underworld in company with others. Nor did I go underground unprepared. I took two spare bulbs for the cap lamp and candle and matches if all else failed. However, these were in a haversack which I had put down to photograph stalactite formations in the upper cave level of Giant's Hole, near Castleton in Derbyshire, England.

When the lamp failed a second time (a shop in error had sold me 2.5amp bulbs instead of the requested 3.5s, and at the time, I didn't notice the difference), I was plunged into darkness.

I felt around but could not find the haversack. So I abandoned the search and headed off in utter darkness along the upper chamber in the direction of the ravine and its stream before losing all sense of direction.

I felt my way along the left side of the upper level and soon was rewarded by hearing the stream tinkling far off and below. I tried to find and cross the rocky parapet bridging the ravine, which had a rope rigged on the other side, but instead slipped over the edge and fell into what I can only describe as another state.

Like others who have had a near-death experience, I found myself floating free with no consciousness of my body. (Others say they could look back down at their body as they travelled from it, but this did not happen to me on this occasion, though I remember that it did when I was much younger, in hospital and in delirium and had what I now see as my first NDE).

Neither did I see recognisable features in my surroundings. In the blackness of deep darkness which exists in caves, you wouldn't expect to, would you? However, it is recorded that totally blind people in their normal life can actually 'see' in their near-death experience. They see their own life replayed before them, realise they are journeying through a dark tunnel, then 'see' Beings of light. Sadly, their new-found faculty of sight is often lost again when they return to their body.

It's important to emphasise that the near-death experience is both real and verifiable. Those who have had out-of-body experiences as part of their NDE, saw identifiable features of the operating room they were in, places, streets and parts of buildings they had not previously visited. In retelling their experience, they could accurately describe features they had only seen when 'out of the body'.

One astounding NDE is that of Dr George Rodonaia, a former Russian research psychiatrist with a Ph.D. in neuropathology and another in the psychology of religion. Until his NDE, he was a determined atheist. In 1976, while still in Russia, he was hit by a car and left for dead in a mortuary for three days. It was only when a pathologist, conducting a post-mortem, cut into his abdomen, that Rodonaia returned to life and cried out from the sudden pain inflicted on him. His sudden and unexpected awakening struck fear and horror into the pathologist and his helpers, who, one suspects, were now as much in need of medical help as their patient.

So, what happened to George during his three days of apparent death? According to the account of his NDE given in Philip L. Berman's book *'The Journey Home'*, he left his body and went into total darkness, wondering how he could still be alive after death. He then tried to think positively in a bid to escape the darkness and find light. As he did so, a bright light appeared, and he saw personified what he calls, 'the universal form of life and nature'. There ensued a holographic drama of his life in review. He became ecstatic as he was filled with 'great knowledge' that included travelling back in time to 'live inside' the minds of Jesus, his disciples and other great figures of history.

Then suddenly, he found himself back in his body and, as said, in serious pain with his belly being cut open. After recovery, he embarked on a new life, taking a second doctorate in religious psychology and, while still in Russia, becoming a priest in the Eastern Orthodox Church. Later, after immigrating to America in 1989, he was appointed pastor at St. Paul United Methodist Church, Baywater, Texas.

Some change for a man who once denied both God and the afterlife, and what a witness to the considerable change a near-death encounter with God can work in the human heart!

Chapter 3 -
THREE NDErs
TELL THEIR STORIES

Now, there are several books telling of near-death experiences. Many feature the stories of atheists and agnostics who found God, unbelievers who met Christ; even some who had committed suicide but found a forgiving God and were returned to bodily life. Others met relatives and some encountered saints of the Bible. None wanted to leave the place of peace and joy they had come to. Here are some of their stories:

Don Brubaker

In Life broadcaster Don Brubaker was mostly too busy to think about death or God, but that changed when he had his own NDE. Clinically dead for 45 minutes, he says he experienced both the glory of heaven and the fire of hell. In his book, *'Absent from the Body'*, he tells of leaving his body and travelling down a tunnel. Panicking, he finds himself in 'hell', but God tells him not to fear because he has been chosen to experience hell and warn others about it. Don is then drawn into 'a vast flaming oven' filled with people laughing because they are not yet hurt by the flames. Alone again, God makes him aware of all the people he was angry with or hurt in life. He then rises to a blue sky and Christ appears in shining light. He is taken back in time to see the Lord's crucifixion, and is then given a choice to stay or return to earthly life.

Dr Richard Eby

Dr Eby, a professor and successful obstetrician, fell off a balcony onto his head. In his book, *'Caught Up Into Paradise'*, he says he found himself out of his body and heard Jesus say, 'Dick, you're dead'. He then asks Jesus many questions, but the Lord responds by saying, 'Didn't you read my book?'- i.e., the Bible. Jesus then answers Richard's questions from Scripture. After this, Richard is led to explore the paradise 'Jesus has prepared for him'. Meanwhile, however, back on earth, his wife is praying for his return, and eventually, Richard, having failed to find her in the afterlife, comes back to her by returning to his body on earth.

Angie Fenimore

Overwhelmed by childhood abuse and adult despair, Angie took her own life in a bid to escape suffering. Her resultant NDE took her into a darkness of hell she describes as more horrific and personal than the 'hellfire and brimstone' mentioned in the Bible. Despite having committed suicide, an 'unforgiveable sin' in some Christians' view, she found that in the afterlife, God cut short the process of her self-immolation. In her book, *'Beyond the Darkness,'* she says God asked her if ending her life was what she really wanted. She complained life was so hard. God responded: 'You think that was hard. It's nothing compared to what awaits if you take your own life. Life is supposed to be hard. You can't skip over parts; what you have earned, you must receive'. But then Jesus appears, and speaking to her of his crucifixion, says, 'I have done this for you'. Jesus pleads her case with God, and she becomes one with Him (that is, with Christ). She is then shown what her future would have been had she completed her suicide. She would have gone to a place where none hear or see God because they do not seek Him, just as they did not seek to know Him in their earthly life. As she gains more light, she is lifted from darkness and returned to her body.

Angie's story raises the question: Is there forgiveness for sins after death? I believe there is or, should I say, there can be. First, because nearly all who have an NDE, have their lives reviewed and amended and are then welcomed in temporary acceptance by 'Beings of Light', who I take to be God the Father and his Son Jesus Christ. Seemingly, the NDEers' sins up to that point are forgiven. Second, because Jesus Himself talked about it:

> *Therefore, I say unto you, every sin and blasphemy will be forgiven men but the blasphemy against the Holy Spirit will not be forgiven men. Anyone who speaks a word against the Son of Man it will be forgiven him; but whoever speaks against the Holy Spirit, it will not be forgiven him either in this age or the age to come.... But I say unto you for every idle word men may speak, they will give account of it in the day of judgement.[2]*

Notice what Jesus said. All sin except that against the Holy Spirit will be forgiven, but the sin against the Holy Spirit will not be forgiven, neither in this age nor in that to come. Doesn't that clearly imply that for other sins, there is forgiveness in the life (age) to come? Note, too, that Jesus further defines the age to

---

[2] Matthew 12:31-32 and 36

come as *'the day of judgement'*. And, for sure, every near-death experiencer undergoes the judgement of a life review in which he or she receives the *'deeds done in the body… whether good or bad'*.[3]

But, and it's an important 'but', I and other NDErs were clearly shown acceptance, peace and the joy of forgiveness, as well. We were shown not only our sins, but what our life could and would be like if our sins were washed away and the righteous life of another – the Holy One Jesus – was set in our place. Remember, *'God is not willing that any should perish but that all should come to repentance'*.[4]

On what basis then can God forgive in the afterlife? Answer: The same ground He employs to forgive all who come to Christ in their earthly life. That when they confess their sins, He is faithful and just to forgive them and cleanse them from all unrighteousness.[5] Believing that Christ died for our sins and rose again to make us right with God and to give us new life, brings total forgiveness. Furthermore, it is clear that, amazing though it is, God readily forgives sins committed in ignorance. Did Jesus not cry out on the cross, *'Father, forgive them for they know not what they do'*?[6]

And doesn't Paul, who as Saul persecuted Jesus' Jewish disciples unto death, as recorded in the Book of Acts, say that when Jesus appeared to him in blazing light on the road to Damascus he was immediately forgiven because of his ignorance? As he explains:

---

[3] 2 Corinthians 5:10
[4] 2 Peter 3:9
[5] 1 John 1:9
[6] Luke 23:34

> *... I was formerly a blasphemer, a persecutor and an insolent man, but I obtained mercy because I did it ignorantly in unbelief. And the grace of our Lord was exceeding abundant with faith and love which are in Christ Jesus (AMP).*[7]

Forgiveness was so instant for Paul, then called Saul, that he was then and there made a minister by Jesus and commissioned as the apostle to the Gentiles.[8]

Now, few seem to realise it, but Paul's Damascus Road conversion was certainly a trance and vision, if not a partial NDE. How so? Well, first up, the light he saw was from heaven *'...brighter than the [noon day, summer] sun shining around me...'*[9] And isn't this the same light we see at the very heart of our near-death experience?

Second, he and his companions *'all fell to the ground'*. In other words, they were temporarily knocked out. Third, Saul heard a voice speaking to him, as NDErs do; fourth, he was left blind by the experience, and fifth, he describes the whole happening as *'a heavenly vision'*[10].

Actually, as will be better explained in a later chapter, one does not have to be near death to have a trance or see a vision. And those that do have such occurrences, definitely do see and experience things from the 'other world' or *'age to come'*.

Indeed, Paul later describes being in a trance when praying in the temple at Jerusalem and seeing a vision of Jesus. *'I was in a trance and saw Him (Jesus) saying to me, "Make haste and get*

---

[7] 1 Timothy 1:13-14
[8] Acts 26:15-18
[9] Acts 26:13-14
[10] Acts 26:19

out of Jerusalem quickly, for they will not receive your testimony concerning Me'.[11]

---

[11] Acts 22:17-18

Chapter 4 -
THE MAN WHO COULDN'T TELL

I must admit, that looking back on my own NDE, I find myself like the *'man'* the Apostle Paul tells about in his second epistle to the Corinthians (chapter 12: 1-4). Paul *'couldn't tell'* whether the man - most likely himself – was *'in the body'* or out of it. What the apostle did know was that *'such an one'* was *'caught up to the third heaven'* and *'heard unspeakable words which it is not lawful for a man to utter'*. Meaning, I take it, words too sacred to be uttered. Or, perhaps, so profound he couldn't express them in everyday language.

Like Paul, I at first did not know whether I had been 'out of the body' or not. Gradually, however, as my memory recalled further details, it became clear that I had indeed been awarded an 'OBE'; no, not the Order of the British Empire, but a genuine 'out-of-body experience'. Granted, at the time, I was unaware of my body, because the utter blackness of the cave meant I couldn't see it. Consequently, it was hard to tell whether I had been out of the body or not. At least not until the NDE was over. Then I knew I was back in my body because of the sudden and tremendous pain I felt.

For the most part, while in 'the other state' – a term used for want of better words to describe it - I experienced much the same sensations commonly reported by NDErs. They are summarised in brief by psychologist and author Kenneth Ring[12], who has studied hundreds of such occurrences, as:

1. Peace
2. Separation
3. Entering, or being in, darkness
4. Seeing a light
5. Encountering or entering the light
6. Being returned to one's body.

Wikipaedia has a more extensive list of occurrences reported by those who have had a near-death experience. They include:

- An awareness of being dead.

- A sense of peace, wellbeing and painlessness. Positive emotions. A sense of removal from the world.

- An *out-of-body experience*, a perception of one's body from an outside position, sometimes observing medics performing resuscitation.

- A 'tunnel' experience, or entering a darkness. A sense of moving upwards along a passageway or staircase.

- Rapid movement toward and/or sudden immersion in a powerful light, or 'Being of Light', which in some cases communicates with the NDE person.

- An intense feeling of *unconditional love and acceptance.*

- Encountering 'beings of light', or dressed in white. Also, in some cases, the hope of being reunited with loved ones.

- Receiving a life 'review', commonly said to be 'seeing one's life flash before your eyes'.

---

[12] Ring, K. (1980). Life at death: A scientific investigation of the near-death experience. New York: Coward, McCann, & Geoghegan., p. 40

- Approaching a border (in my case, beyond which I could not go), then either deciding to go back to one's body (or, in my case, being forcibly taken back to it).
- Suddenly finding oneself 'back in one's body'.

Like many others, I found the near-death experience profound and beautiful. It opened the way into another realm where peace, joy and warm, non-judgmental acceptance abounded. If this was the afterlife, then it seemed there was nothing to be frightened of. There was no chilling judgement and punishment of my life to date and its sins, which were already many.

Nor was there even a hint of a fiery, eternal hell or the grim 'Judgement Day' I had been so often warned about by the stern, black-suited Calvinist ministers of my upbringing in the Strict and Particular Baptist chapels of England. (In passing, if the name 'Strict and Particular' sounds off-putting, believe me, it doesn't begin to describe the actuality).

An important point to note, is that at no time during my out of body experience, did I fear or anticipate death; rather, I was caught up in the sensations of the wonderful things that were being opened up to me. Perhaps this is because my NDE happened suddenly and immediately upon my fall in the cave. Other NDErs report fearing death, but they were seriously ill or were on the operating table when they had their NDE – so death or the possibility of death was already in their consciousness.

But, I repeat, at no stage of my NDE, did death or the approach of it form part of my awareness. Rather I was being given entry into a wonderful and far better world or state of experience and simply couldn't get enough of it. Later, however, back in my body and once again facing earthly life with all its limitations, I found this lack of fear about death continued. So much so, that it baffled some well-meaning relatives and friends who earnestly sought to 'win me to Christ' and get me 'saved' when I told them I had no fear of dying because I had already experienced that.

'But you could die and go to hell', they warned. 'But I already died and it wasn't like that at all', I replied. 'Rather, it was beautiful; there was no flaming fire or devil with a red-hot pitchfork to prod me. Instead, there was love joy, peace from beautiful Beings of Light'. This was too much for them, of course. They were too polite to say so out loud, but privately concluded I was deluded.

However, on one point, that I needed to be saved, they were correct. And years later, I was led to submit to Christ as Saviour and Lord, not out of fear of death, but because I needed to be saved out of the mess I had made of my life. And it was the same people, principally my cousin Eileen and her husband George, who were instrumental in my conversion. Their one plea was that in coming to Christ I did not become 'religious or churchy' but get to know Jesus personally through his word, the Bible. It's something I try hard to live up to, today.

In reviewing my NDE episode, I recall there was a vivid sensation of being 'lifted up and away'. However, I could not confirm that visually because I couldn't look back down on my body, for the simple reason I and the cave were in impenetrable darkness.

As this ascent occurred, it seemed I was also seized deep in my being with a strong desire to escape from the black confines of my 'dark' personal and spiritual existence to date. The impression gained from the dark 'tunnel' through which I was travelling was that it was a way of escape from a state of extreme smallness. The only life I had known to this point, of myself, my home, parents, school and surrounding countryside, and my very limited perception of it, now appeared tiny in comparison to greater vistas of understanding seemingly offered by the light glimpsed ahead.

I could not have put it into words back then, but it was brought home to me how minute my outlook and knowledge was. Now, however, I can say that from deep within me as I lay unconscious in the cave, there surfaced a powerful urge to escape my narrow 'tunnel vision' and experience vistas of understanding far wider than I knew.

I then felt I was being shown an entrance into a huge other world of great experience and understanding, in which things didn't go wrong as they so often did in mine. In this 'other world', it seemed there was no horizon, no boundaries were set, no rules had to be obeyed; there were no failures, no setbacks. Rather, there was complete freedom to explore, to go forth, to expand one's understanding in an unending vista of enlightening experience that spoke loud and clear that, above all else, it was, and would be, nothing but GOOD. This because it was all of God.

By contrast, all I had known to date was a childhood which, while happy at times, was largely beset with my own awkwardness and the difficulties my parents had. Mum was a cripple, depressed and angry at having had her leg amputated and subsequently struggling to walk. Dad was often ill and hospitalised for varicose veins and other complaints.

We experienced poverty as Dad's attempted business ventures failed and he became too ill to work. I was sent to live with relatives for two years because Mum's emotional and mental state apparently made it unsafe for me to be with her. In the post-Second-World-War years, as we moved from place to place, Dad struggled to find work and at times, we had little to eat. By the time of my caving trauma, however, things were somewhat better, and we were living in Rochdale, Lancashire, where my father was a part-time chapel caretaker and, when able, worked as a plumber.

Summarising my cave NDE experience, like others, I felt myself being drawn through a dark tunnel, then glimpsed a light in the distance. And, far from this 'light at the end of tunnel' being 'a train coming the other way', as the cynical saying has it, the light was warm and beautiful. Above all, it gave me an incredible feeling of peace. It was as though all striving and struggling had ceased. More than that, there was a sense of having arrived and being 'at home' in a place of great spiritual blessing.

Without being told so, I sensed that this was the rightful and proper destiny of every person, and on reflection much later was saddened to realise most of us are ignorant of its existence for most of our earthly lives.

Chapter 5 -
THE MISSED MESSAGE OF NDE

It's amazing how blind we human beings can be. Even when the obvious stares us in the face, we refuse to accept it and choose to believe something else instead. Often the truth is hidden in plain sight, yet we ignore it and draw an opposite and wrong conclusion. To counter this tendency this chapter looks afresh at the near-death experience to see what the vast majority of participants and commentators on it seem to have missed.

Fact is, that because they are so entranced by the sheer bliss of the near-death experience, many who have undergone it, myself included at the time, take away a false hope from the occurrence, one which denies the essential lesson it is teaching. You see, for many years after my brush with death and entry into the world beyond this life, I lived in a state of happy ignorance, blithely assuming that when I finally die, I would once again be escorted into the realm of bliss I had encountered in the cave, only this time to stay forever.

But the essential meaning to be taken from the NDE is that all who go through it are returned from this far happier realm to their limited and more miserable bodily existence on earth. Granted, some choose to come back when presented with a choice on the matter. But by far the large majority of NDErs are forcibly conducted back down the dark tunnel to awake in the body they earlier left.

And while not a few radically change their life and seek God or at least improve their behaviour as a result, many, myself included back then, take false hope from the experience. Thus, I wrongly thought that at my eventual demise there would be a return to the bliss I had briefly encountered in my cave NDE. And this would be achieved, I thought, without need for a Saviour who had shed his blood for me or the need for me to repent of the many sinful things I had done.

But, again, how wrong can you be? For the real NDE message is that all who return to earthly life have been clearly rejected as unfit to stay in the joyful realm they briefly visit. Sure, both they and I sampled what a blessed abode it is, but we were then judged, weighed and found too wanting to remain. How could I possibly have ignored this sentence of dismissal and believed instead, that in experiencing near death, I had received a ticket and passport to glory? More than that, how could millions of others have missed it, too?

So, the question every surviving NDEr should ask is: How can I qualify for this life beyond the present life? What do I have to do to be received in that place when my body finally dies? But you will peruse in vain many books about near-death experiences to find such a question posed, still less answered. Nor do most such writings address the issue of just what part of us, when we are near dead, is able to sense, feel, know vastly more than we did before and enter into ecstasy in the afterlife. It's a vital question because, while many believe it is the soul that will live on in an afterlife, the medical determination is that it cannot.

For the record, the soul is understood to be the mind and, as such, the expression of our will and emotions. How, psychiatrists and psychologists ask, can the mind of a near-death, unconscious person still operate when they are brain dead? They then confess themselves at a loss to provide an adequate answer.

In his intriguing book, *'Nothing Better Than Death'*, near-death experiencer and author Kevin R. Williams asserts that: 'Scientists do not know enough about consciousness; they cannot define or locate it'. For example, for years, psychiatrist, physician and Freudian analyst, Dr. Stanislav Grof,[13] who has had 'powerful mystical experiences' himself, believed our self-awareness was 'hard-wired in the brain'.

Today, however, he is quite sure it comes instead from a cosmic source that 'lies beyond time and space'. He notes the Latin word *persona,* from which we derive the word 'person', means a mask. And the mask we wear is our physically self-conscious identity. At death, or in near death, this mask is removed, he asserts, for our conscious personality 'dies along with the brain'.

He posits that with no brain to 'reduce' our consciousness, our consciousness expands and so a new personality emerges. Accordingly, when a person is revived from an NDE, it is suggested the brain's 'reducing valve', as postulated by Dr. Grof, begins to work again and the old personality reappears, though drastically changed.

His resultant theory is that the brain actually reduces or limits our consciousness to create our personality. From this, Kevin Williams proposes that upon death the brain dies and our consciousness is forever changed, 'as it expands into the cosmic consciousness'.[14] But is this the whole truth? I think not.

---

[13] See his website.

[14] Kevin R. Williams, *'Nothing Better Than Death',* published by Xlibris Corporation, USA, 2002, pages 154-155, used by permission

Also missed by many, is the question of how a vast increase in knowledge of themselves, of reality, of the future, of another world altogether and of their own potential, is imparted to many NDErs? It cannot be from the brain if that is dead, neither can it be through the emotions since they are stimulated by the brain's amygdala which also would not be functioning. Nor can it be via a person's will (decision-making ability) since the near-death trip is an involuntary imposed experience and the brain is defunct. A later chapter will seek to provide the true answer.

As to why one is shown such wonderful knowledge, is the reason merely to prompt us to try in our own strength to become the far better person that in our NDE we were shown we could become? Or is it to cause us to repent, believe in God and thus realise through faith in Him (not in our own works) the great destiny that He has already prepared for those who trust Him?

Beyond that, is the big question of how to fit one's near-death experience into the personal picture one has of reality. Is it a one-off, out-of-the-blue blunder into a trance that may be a delusion? Or is it a journey into another, spiritual dimension that is far more real and true than our present, fraught existence in our earthly body? More questions that remain to be answered after an NDE are:

1) How shall we then live what is left of our lives in the here and now?

2) How can we prepare for eventual death knowing what we now know as a result of the NDE?

These important questions and messages will be addressed in more detail in subsequent chapters.

Chapter 6 -
PROOF OF AN AFTERLIFE?

So, what is the truth about near-death experiences? Are they proof of an afterlife? And, if so, is *'Life After Life'*, as one book title puts it, full of light, peace and joy, or is it a figment of one's imagination? And, if there is a place of peace and light for us after death, is it for everyone, or just a few?

It would be a bitter disappointment, should I be able to experience it, if at my eventual bodily decease, I again briefly experience the love, joy and peace of Beings who know no evil and live in apparent happiness far above the darkness of this world, only to be dragged away to die, to go into that 'long dark night', as one poet described it, and thus simply cease to be. Or worse still, live on only to miss out on heaven and go to a hell of self-imposed torment instead.

Now it is true, as has been rightly pointed out, that the individual perception of such NDE experiences is strongly influenced, and perhaps sometimes dictated by, the recipient's cultural and religious beliefs, particularly when it comes to later interpreting what happened. It becomes necessary then to examine all the research, knowledge and conclusions that exist about the phenomenon.

Accordingly, this book considers the scientific, medical and psychological studies of the phenomenon, looks at spiritual or transcendental theories about it and critiques other purported explanations as to what NDE actually is. In particular, it tests claims that it has a physiological or psychiatric source.

Later, the author will set out his own conclusions which include a rational yet ancient understanding of the experience, as recorded in mankind's earliest documents and, which, to the best of his knowledge, has not been fully set forth to date in the debate that has raged about NDE for the last 50 years.

Also to be addressed, is the popular belief advanced by the best-selling book *'Life After Life'*[15] that there is indeed an afterlife, and that NDE is proof of it regardless of what one believes or does. The author, Dr. Raymond Moody, who had a near-death experience himself, while attempting to commit suicide (as a result of his mind being affected by thyroid illness), evidently believes more in reincarnation than the biblical doctrine of resurrection.

A former forensic psychiatrist at a Georgia, USA, mental hospital, he maintains he has had nine lives previous to his current one. Nevertheless, he is right in saying, after extensive research:

> *I don't mind saying that after talking with over a thousand people who have had these experiences, and having experienced many times some of the really baffling and unusual features of these experiences, it has given me great confidence that there is a life after death. As a matter of fact, I must confess to you in all honesty, I have absolutely no doubt, on the basis of what my patients have told me, that they did get a glimpse of the beyond.*

---

[15]Raymond A. Moody 2001, *Life After Life*, (foreword by Elizabeth Kubler-Ross), Random House.

Now he's certainly right that there is a world beyond. However, following publication of his book, Dr. Moody was wrong when he reinvented 'psychomanteums' to which ancient Greeks resorted to consult apparitions of the dead. (Moody had read about these in classic Greek texts he encountered, while a student at the University of Virginia). To further pursue an occult experience of the 'afterlife', Moody built a 'psychomanteum' in Alabama, which he called the 'Dr. John Dee Memorial Theater of the Mind'.

By staring into a mirror in a dimly lit room, Moody claims that people visiting the psychomanteum are able to summon up visions of spiritual apparitions. Moody has also researched 'past life regression', a technique that uses hypnosis to recover what practitioners believe are memories of past lives or incarnations.

It needs to be said that Moody's conclusions about the 'afterlife', occult and New Age as they are, have been strongly challenged by both psychologists and philosophers. For example, noted psychology professor Barry Beyerstein deems Moody's alleged evidence for an afterlife 'flawed, both logically and empirically'[16]. Psychologist James Alcock has noted that Moody '...appears to ignore a great deal of the scientific literature dealing with hallucinatory experiences in general, just as he quickly glosses over the very real limitations of his research method.'[17]

---

[16] Barry Beyerstein. (1990). *Evaluating the Anomalous Experience*. In Kendrick Frazier. *The Hundredth Monkey and Other Paradigms of the Paranormal*. Prometheus Books. pp. 43–53. ISBN 0-87975-655-1.

[17] James Alcock. (1981). *Psychology and Near-Death Experiences*. In Kendrick Frazier. *Paranormal Borderlands of Science*. Prometheus Books. pp. 153–69. ISBN 0-87975-148-7.

Philosophers are also scathing. Paul Kurtz maintains, 'there is no reliable evidence that people who report such experiences have died and returned, or that consciousness exists separate from the brain or body.'[18] And Robert Todd Carroll accuses Moody of omitting cases that do not fit his hypothesis. He holds that what Moody describes as a typical NDE may be due to brain states triggered by cardiac arrest and anaesthesia. They can be explained by 'neurochemistry' and are the result of a 'dying, demented or drugged brain', he asserts.[19]

Undoubtedly, a survivable near-death experience is not an event that happens to all, for the simple reason it is only a minority that revive from such a close encounter with death, a happening which otherwise is thought by many to end with entry into 'the long, dark night'. And that's a description with especial meaning for me, given my own NDE occurred in a cave.

Therefore, it remains true that the far more numerous majority who experience NDE actually go on to die and, though they undoubtedly have a near death and actual death experience as a part of their demise, their testimony of how it was for them is lost to us. Contrary to the claims of Dr. Moody, it can be said that, with the notable exception of Jesus, very few speak back to anybody from or after the grave.

It is also important to know that NDE experiences are not the exclusive preserve of adult human beings. They happen to little children, dogs, cats and other animals as well. Rats have been found to have greatly heightened brain activity directly

---

[18] Paul Kurtz. (1991). *Toward a New Enlightenment: The Philosophy of Paul Kurtz.* Transaction Publishers. p. 349. ISBN 1-56000-118-6

[19] Robert Todd Carroll. (2003). *The Skeptic's Dictionary: A Collection of Strange Beliefs, Amusing Deceptions, and Dangerous Delusions.* Wiley. p. 251. ISBN 0-471-27242-6

following cardiac arrest, for example. Unfortunately, no similar research has been conducted on humans.

Furthermore, NDE is world-wide. It is experienced in every culture and race of humankind. And it is ancient. Gregory Shushan[20] has analysed the 'afterlife' of five ancient empires: Old and Middle Kingdom Egypt, Sumeria, Old Babylonian Mesopotamia, Vedic India, pre-Buddhist China and pre-Columbian Meso-America, comparing them with historical and contemporary reports of near-death experiences and supposed Shamanic 'afterlife' experiences. He found similarities stretching far across time that cannot be explained by coincidence.

Bruce Greyson[21] asserts that the central features of NDEs are universal and have not been influenced by time. He says they have been observed throughout history and in different cultures. But he, like nearly all researchers into and commentators upon the strange experience, struggles to explain what it means.

But now let's hear the story of one ancient man who wrote a book to tell us of how he really died and then came back to life, once again by a 'miracle in the dark':

---

[20] Shushan, Gregory (2009). *Conceptions of the After Life in Early Civilisations: Universalism, Constructivism, and Near-death experiences.* London: Continuum. ISBN 978 -0-8264-4073-0.
[21] Bruce Greyson is the Chester F. Carlson Professor of Psychiatry and Neurobehavioral Sciences and Director of the Division of Perceptual Studies at the University of Virginia Medical School, a founding member of the International Association for Near-Death Studies (IANDS), has written two books and has edited the *Journal of Near-Death Studies* for the better part of three decades.

Chapter 7 -
INSIDE THE BELLY
OF THE FISH

I'm a voice from the past but not from the grave. For, you see, I'm now in a far better place than the grave. I'm in Paradise, in the presence of God and awaiting resurrection back on earth in that special day when the Messiah shines forth his glory on earth - the day of Christ[22] - and resurrects Israel's saints back to bodily life as He has promised to do.

And it's just as well I'm not still on earth, seeing that Muslim Shiites have now destroyed my actual grave and body anyway.[23] Actually, such earthly sacrilege concerns me little. What worries me more is the ongoing, unrelenting academic refusal to believe my story is real. And this even by Christian scholars, so-called.

So, I'm speaking out to set the record straight and reaffirm that my own 'miracle in the dark', that of dying in the belly of a fish and being raised to life again, is true. Of course, it is said the dead cannot (and, in the view of many, therefore should not) speak, but I feel I am allowed

---

[22] 1 Corinthians 1:8, Philippians 1:6; 2:10 and 16.
[23] Al-Sumeria news reported July 27 2014 that ISIS (radical Islamic State of Iraq and Syria) militants had destroyed Jonah's tomb and shrine in Iraq's northern city of Mosul. The Prophet Younis (Jonah) was highly revered by both Christians and Muslims, the report noted.

to address you because my story is recorded in the Bible for all to read. So also, is that of righteous but murdered Abel. And, if Abel can *still speak though dead'*,[24] then perhaps I can be allowed to do so, too.

Now, you will know me as Jonah. Most everybody does, even if they haven't read the Bible. What you don't know is the answer to a riddle that for thousands of years has puzzled the brightest of biblical scholars who have read my book, the Book of Jonah in the Bible. In short it is this: How is it I could pray to God while in the belly of the fish when actually I was dead?

The answer is important not only to understand what a person may undergo in death but also to realise the overlooked truth that underlies a near-death experience. But first, let me tell you more about me, for my earthly life is a cautionary tale. You would do well to learn from it to avoid the unpleasant consequences of my refusal to forgive, prejudice and disobedience that landed me in so much trouble.

Perhaps, as I was, you are one earmarked to be saved by God and chosen to carry out an important mission for Him. If so, I beg you to listen to His voice and mine. Even, and especially, if His voice requires you to repent and forgive those you hate.

Now, in my life on earth, I was a prophet, son of the Prophet Amittai whose name means 'truth of the Lord'. I was born in Gath-Hepher, which means 'as prophesied'. My own name means 'Dove' or 'peace'. Born in the eighth century BC I lived on into the seventh.

---

[24] Hebrews 11:4

Evidence of my prophetic office is that scripture records that King Jeroboam, son of Joash, *'restored the coast of Israel from entering in of Hamath unto the sea of the plain, according to the word of the Lord God of Israel which He spake by the hand of his servant Jonah...'*[25]

So, I was prophesying long before God told me to go and cry against the wickedness of that great city Nineveh, capital of the Assyrian empire[26]. But, as you may have read, I refused to go and fled from my home in Israel and from *'the presence of the Lord'.*[27] In fact, I paid to board a ship sailing from Joppa (today's Tel Aviv) to the furthest outpost known to me, Tarshish in Spain. That would have been a voyage of some 2,500 miles had not God interrupted it. By contrast, Nineveh was some 725 miles from Joppa in the opposite direction.

As you know, God sent a storm that so terrified the ship's crew they eventually heaved me over the side. Ever since, to sailors, I have been the legendary 'Jonah' that would doom any voyage just by being aboard ship. In the upshot, far from succeeding in running from God and avoiding the mission He required of me, I was taken homewards inside a great fish. And it is how I fared inside that creature's belly that throws light on both the near-death and actual death experience this book discusses. From the tale I emerge as one of the very few people, apart from Jesus Christ, to have suffered death and been brought back to life to tell others about it.

---

[25] 2 Kings 14:25
[26] Jonah 1:1
[27] Jonah 1:2

First though, I must explain why I fled from God's presence and His appointed task, and to understand that you need to know a little history. We Israelites hated Assyrians with good cause. They were our most feared enemy. In 722BC they conquered Israel destroying our capital, Samaria. Just 21 years later they nearly conquered Jerusalem, the capital of Judah.

But the main cause of our hatred was their terrible cruelty. They rejoiced in amputating hands and feet, gouging eyes, skinning and impaling their captives while still alive. As the Prophet Nahum later said, *'Who has not felt your endless cruelty?'*[28] Reliefs in Nineveh's palace, the ruins of which have been found by archaeologists, show people being impaled, decapitated, flayed, and their tongues pulled out.

Thus, the very thought of giving the *'bloody city'* a chance to repent was repugnant to me. And though I eventually, but still reluctantly, obeyed the Lord and warned Nineveh of its impending doom, I was very angry when He actually spared the city from destruction. As it is written of me:

> *He prayed to the Lord, 'O Lord is not this what I said when I was still at home? That is why I was so quick to flee to Tarshish. I knew that you are a gracious and compassionate God, slow to anger and abounding in love, a God who relents from sending calamity. Now O Lord take away my life. For it is better for me to die than to live.*[29]

---

[28] Nahum 3:19

[29] Jonah 4:1-3

It's annoying that, had I only lived a few years longer, I would have seen with my earthly eyes God's prophesied judgement fall on Nineveh anyway. That took place in 612BC.[30] For although the Assyrians for a time repented at my prophesied warning, later they resumed their proud and wicked ways. My successor, the Prophet Nahum, accurately predicted their final doom:

> *Horsemen charge with bright sword and glittering spear. There is a multitude of slain, a great number of bodies, countless corpses—they stumble over the corpses.*[31]

As for me, I had to learn the hard way that God is *'gracious and compassionate...slow to anger and abounding in love'.*[32] And that means He will spare and save any person or nation who repents (i.e., changes their mind and behaviour and turns to God) no matter who they are or what they have done, short of blaspheming the Holy Spirit.

Was God's way of changing my mind hard? You'd better believe it. It was a nightmare ride inside the slimy belly of a fish doing its best to digest me as it swam hundreds of miles across the ocean to spew me up on the shores of Israel, putting me back en route to Nineveh.

Now many Bible scholars dismiss my story as legend. They call it the myth of 'Jonah and the whale'. But is it? After all, God saw fit to include it in the Bible and Jesus Himself treated it as solid fact. What's more, He recounts an important detail found in my book, the Book of Jonah.

---

[30] Nahum 2:13, 3:4
[31] Nahum 3:3
[32] Exodus 34:6

It is that I was in the fish's belly for *'...three days and three nights.'*

Now, I didn't know how long I was held in the fish's stomach. I didn't have a watch and there was nothing but night and no way to count time in there. But centuries later when the Jewish Pharisees and law teachers asked Jesus to show them a miraculous sign He said:

> *A wicked and adulterous generation asks for a miraculous sign. But none will be given unto it except the sign of the Prophet Jonah. For as Jonah was three days and three nights in the belly of a huge fish, so the Son of Man will be three days and three nights in the heart of the earth.*[33]

Here the Lord clearly foretold He would die, be buried and then rise to life again. And I'm happy my own experience was a pointer to the death He died and to the resurrection now hoped for by those who put their trust in Him. Importantly, Jesus's own death and resurrection confirms essential truths about my own experience.

Firstly, that like Him I really did die, but inside the fish, not on a cross. You see, there was no air to breathe in the creature's belly, so I quickly suffocated. And once I was dead the creature's gastric juices got to work on me. As my book says in Jonah 2:6 what happened to me was *'corruption'*; my body was rotting away.

Thus, after 72 hours of slow digestion, my outer layers were already eaten away. Thankfully, at the time, I wasn't alive – as some have claimed – to be aware of this. But, amazingly, though dead, I was aware of God and, as my book says, I prayed to Him out of the fish's belly:

---

[33] Matthew 12:40

In my distress I called to the Lord and He answered me. From the depths of the grave, I called for help and You listened to my cry.[34]

In Hebrew the words translated *'from the depths of the grave'* are literally *'from the belly of Sheol'*, meaning that while in the fish I went to the realm of the dead. Here's what that felt like:

*The waters compassed me about even to the extinction of life; the abyss surrounded me; the seaweed was wrapped about my head. I went down to the bottoms and the very roots of the mountains; the earth with its bars closed behind me **forever**. Yet You have brought up my life from the pit and **corruption,** O Lord my God. (AMP)* [35]

You see, I really did die and, in the verses above, I tell you what that really was like. It was awful. So, for me to come back from there to life, healed and whole was a miracle. Truly a 'miracle in the dark'. But you might ask, how was I able to pray to God when dead? The short answer is that I did so through my spirit, for the spirit lives on after death. What's more, it is the spirit of a person that leaves the body in a near-death experience and enters, albeit briefly, the realm of light.

Shortly, this book will examine scriptural and other evidence for the spirit living on after death but first, let me, Jonah, as one who has been there, say clearly that it is not one's soul but one's spirit - and only one's spirit - which journeys out of the body into the realm of light in both the death and near-death experience.

---

[34] Jonah 2:2
[35] Jonah 2:5-6

You see, in the face of death my soul *'fainted upon me [crushing me]* (AMP).[36] In other words, my soul died, but that was not the end for me. *'When my soul fainted (died) within me, I remembered the Lord and my prayer went up to You, into your holy temple.'[37]*

The big lesson I learned out of it all was obedience. That when God says 'go', you must go and do what He says. And, may I say, that if you are not obeying Him now, then turn around and ask Him to forgive you for your sin and help you obey Him from now on. As a spirit now living with Him in the afterlife, I know that already, God, as Jesus, has bled and died Himself to take the punishment for sin that you and I deserved. All so that we don't have to forego being with Him when we die.

---

[36] Jonah 2:7
[37] Jonah 2:7

Chapter 8 -
LIVING ON AFTER DEATH

So, why do so many NDErs and the neurologists and psychologists who study the phenomenon believe it is the soul that lives on even when the brain is dead? Answer: They do not believe the Bible truth that it is only one's spirit that survives death to return to God to be accountable *'for the deeds done in the body'*[38] Doesn't Ecclesiastes 12:7 say that the dust (of our body) returns to earth but *'...the spirit will return to God who gave it'*?

Against that truth the philosopher Plato held that it was only one's soul that lived on in an after-life. Seemingly, he knew nothing of the spirit. And in a recent book *'The Secret Second Coming'* medium Patricia Doyle invokes what she calls *'A Second New Testament'* to assert that the 'whole idea of Jesus dying on the cross for our sins is untrue'.

Sadly, the bogus *'New Testament'* she trusts is based on the 'spirit writings' of a 19th century séance attender James Padgett who, though ostensibly a Christian, claimed that through automatic writing 'Jesus', 'John', and other biblical figures dictated letters to him correcting the 'many errors' in the commonly accepted Bible. Take this blasphemy for a sample: 'The great gift of God to man was not Jesus but the potentiality of obtaining the Divine Love of the Father and thus becoming divine and fitted to reside in the mansions of heaven', he asserts.

---

[38] 2 Corinthians 5:10

How that can be done without the help of Jesus as our Redeemer, escapes me. And from Doyle's supposed 'Apostle John': 'The pity of it all is that mortals for all these long years have believed they were saved by his sacrifice and blood and by such belief have never come any nearer to the Master or at-one-ment with the Father.'

Padgett and Doyle are far from believing what the Bible actually says. Indeed, they claim 'Jesus' told them his own recorded teaching - that only the converted are the sons of God - is 'a damnable and harmful doctrine'.

It isn't, of course, but the Doyle-Padgett teaching certainly is. So, when it comes to whether it is one's soul or one's spirit that enters realms beyond in near death, it's no surprise that Padgett, Doyle and the 'Jesus' they say spoke to them mentions only the soul. Though scripture clearly teaches '...*the soul that sinneth it shall die*' [39] they maintain it can somehow enter and stay in the heavenly courts with its sin intact.

Thus, they conclude a person can reach heaven without repenting, without trusting Jesus, being baptised, receiving the Holy Spirit, obeying Jesus' written commandments or trusting God's word, the Bible, as absolute truth. In other words, they aver, somehow one's soul can get to heaven without being converted. It comes as no surprise therefore, that their 'Jesus' supposedly says he is not God, did not have a virgin birth, did not die for the world's sins and cannot save people – they must do that for themselves.

So, let's get it straight. What does the Bible actually teach about what happens to us after death? Is it our soul or our spirit that goes into the afterlife either temporarily or for good? Ecclesiastes 12:7 makes clear:

---

[39] Ezekiel 18:4,20

> *Then shall the dust [out of which God made man's body] return to the earth as it was and the **spirit** shall return to God who gave it (AMP).*

In Ezekiel 18:4 and 20 we find verses that twice assert, '*... the soul that sins shall die'.*

What's more, Romans 3:23 says that '*...all have sinned and come short of the glory of God'.* So, you might ask, how can a sinning soul go to be with God after death? The short answer is that it can't. It is the spirit that goes to meet God in that blessed state and is only able to stay on if presented before God as '*...holy and unblameable and unreprovable in his sight'.*[40]

And thereby hangs the problem. Being found faultless before the Lord Jesus Christ and therefore worthy to enter his heavenly kingdom is not something anyone can attain by their own efforts. That is made clear by the passage Romans 3:20-22 which explains how helpless, hopeless sinners can be made right with God. And it's not by channelling spirit messages from the dead or trying in our strength to make ourselves better, as Padgett and Doyle assert. It's something only God can do. And it's called **reconciliation.**

> *For it pleased the Father that in Him (i.e., Christ) should all fullness (of God) dwell. And, having made peace through the blood of his cross, by Him to **reconcile** all things unto Himself ... And you who were sometime alienated and enemies in your mind by wicked works yet now hath He (Christ) **reconciled** in the body of his flesh through death to present you holy and unblameable and unreprovable in his sight (AMP).*[41]

---

[40] Colossians 1:22
[41] Colossians 1: 19-22.

Short of surrender to the Lord Jesus Christ as Saviour and Lord, and his work within us to make us what we should be, there is no way we can qualify to live with God in 'eternity', which is the Bible word for the afterlife. And so, every attempt we make to improve our behaviour through our soul - our mind, our will and our emotions – will be closely scrutinised at the Judgement Seat of Christ which we encounter in our near or actual death experience. As Ecclesiastes 12:14 insists:

> *...God shall bring every work into judgment, with every secret thing, whether it is good or evil.*

But you ask, surely God will give me 'Brownie points' for the good things I have done, helping others, giving to charity and being kind, even if I never followed and obeyed Jesus? Well, no. Not if those deeds were done in our unsaved, unredeemed, unreconciled human nature that ignores or hates God and does not obey Jesus. Romans 8:5-8 bluntly says:

> *Those who live according to the sinful nature (i.e., the flesh) have their minds set on what that nature desires: but those who live in accordance with the Spirit (of Christ) have their minds set on what the Spirit desires. The mind of sinful man is death, but the mind controlled by the Spirit is life and peace. The sinful mind is hostile to God. It does not submit to God's law, nor can it do so. Those controlled by the sinful nature cannot please God (NIV).*

And Jesus Himself told his disciples:

It is the Spirit who gives life [He is the Life-giver]: the flesh (our sinful nature) conveys no benefit whatever [there is no profit in it]. (AMP) 42

So, it should come as no surprise to find that it is only in the spirit that we enter heaven, so to speak, in the near-death experience. But again, there's a problem. When the Apostle Paul had a near-death experience and went to '*Paradise*' in the third heaven [43] it appears he would have met only '*...the spirits of just men made perfect*'.[44] (Please note, it is widely held that Paul wrote both Hebrews and Second Corinthians, both of which refer to near death or after death experiences.) The Amplified Bible puts it more strongly: ... *[you have come] to the God who is judge of all and to the* **spirits** *of the righteous (the redeemed in heaven) who have been made perfect*'.

Now, in our near-death experiences didn't we meet a Holy Judge who sent us back to our earthly life; didn't we also sense and encounter other holy beings and want more than we ever wanted anything to stay with them? And weren't we sent back to our bodies feeling far from perfect? If we can go only in spirit to the realm of peace, we have to ask how we can learn to live in our spirit while still in this life and not just in our flesh, our sinful nature. This, so that we can be found '*alive in the spirit*' when our time of departure comes. Because one thing is already clear: it isn't our soul that can enter heaven as our home; it is our spirit.

---

42 John 6:63
43 2 Corinthians 12:2-5
44 Hebrews 12:23

But again, there's a problem. Right now, short of personal faith and trust in Christ, God counts us as spiritually dead, our spirits slain by our trespasses and sins[45]. What we need is to be 'made alive' again. And, amazingly this is just what God does when we turn to Christ and ask Him to be our Saviour and Lord. Thus Ephesians 2:4-5 says that because of his *great love* for us:

> *...even when we were dead in trespasses (He) has made us alive together with Christ (by grace you have been saved).*

I am convinced that I and other NDErs had their spirit temporarily made alive by God in the near-death experience just so they could taste heaven and have lodged in their hearts the desire to be there permanently. Thus, we were brought to know what it is to float out of the body, move freely, start to know all truth about ourselves, life, God, death and the future, and meet, albeit briefly, holy Beings on the other side. Truly a 'miracle in the dark' that brings light to us in more ways than one.

So, it was in spirit and not in the soul that we tasted the afterlife. But this is not to say that, if we are believers, our ultimate destiny is to remain in the heavenly spirit realm. No. At 'the last day' there will be a resurrection back onto earth and we will then be in what the Apostle Paul calls our *body from heaven*, a physically real but nonetheless 'spiritual body', i.e., one that cannot sin.

And when that happens, we will once again become '*a living soul*'[46] just as Adam did, long ago. For man by definition is composed of spirit, soul and body, the soul being our life which

---

[45] Ephesians 2:1
[46] Genesis 2:7

dies and the spirit that is present after death. Thus, the Apostle Paul prays in 1 Thessalonians 5:23:

> *And may the God of peace Himself sanctify you through and through [separate you from profane things, make you pure and wholly consecrated unto God]: and may your spirit, soul and body be preserved sound and complete [and found] blameless at the coming of our Lord Jesus Christ... (AMP)*

To make us blameless calls for a lifelong series of miracles greater than our NDE which was a miracle in itself. How will God do this in us? Answer: By making our spirit alive again together with his Spirit, the Spirit of Christ, so that it is He who actually lives in us and not we ourselves. For, in 1 Corinthians 6:17 we are told:

> *But the person who is united with Christ becomes one spirit with Him. Shun immorality and all sexual looseness (AMP).*[47]

But how can we be saved and made alive again, our spirits joined with Christ's Spirit? Answer: Through believing Jesus died for our sins and rose again so that we could be quickened (made alive again) and eventually bodily resurrected like Him.[48] We must believe that it is his blood, and only his blood, and no-one else's (not even our own), that cleanses us from all sin and guilt.[49] So faith is the key.

---

[47] 1 Corinthians 17-18

[48] 1 Corinthians 15:4,

[49] 1 John 1:7

But what is faith? It is:

... That leaning of the entire human personality on Him (Christ) in absolute trust in his power, wisdom and goodness. As you therefore received Christ [even] Jesus the Lord [so] walk (regulate your lives and conduct yourselves) in union with and conformity to Him (AMP). [50]

---

[50] Colossians 2:5-6

Chapter 9 -
SO WHO IS IN CHARGE?

An important issue to settle is what or who controls the near-death experience? For, undeniably, the person actually undergoing an NDE is neither able to bring it about nor change the course it takes. Without exception, all NDErs report being taken on a journey without being asked, a journey they feel is ordered and activated by a power beyond themselves. So, who or what is it?

Is the subconscious mind playing out a dream-like drama to sooth and soften the pangs of approaching death? Or, are chemical hallucinations to blame? Neurologists proffer the notion that the NDE is the brain's brave farewell just before it dies but actually doctors have long known that within seconds of the blood supply being cut off the brain shuts down completely.

Yet, patients whose hearts stop on the operating table and thus become effectively brain dead can still see, sense and be conscious of everything that happens to them in their journey to the 'other realm' in the near-death experience. True, the NDE may last only a few minutes before it ends as resuscitation or recovery kicks in but, apparently, that's more than time enough for this profound occurrence to take place.

As an aside, I remember years ago when being driven semi-conscious to hospital with acute appendicitis (it was all but ready to burst) time slowed down. So much so that I could count every drain hole in the kerb as it seemed to crawl past at a snail's pace. So, it should be no surprise that time is hugely distorted if not irrelevant in an NDE. It seems much knowledge can be imparted and eternity sensed in the seconds it takes to enter, no matter how briefly, into the 'other world'.

And, if the person being taken on this journey is in no way responsible for the happening, nor is a chemical or biological reaction, then, again, who or what is? For there is an ordered sequence of events that occurs in almost every NDE. Furthermore, there is a clear use of firm control when NDEers, against their will, are taken back into life in the body as their brief encounter with a realm of ecstasy is brought to an end.

There is power in that expulsion, power that evidently is not open to or subject to human control. It is an inexorable power that cannot be persuaded against its decision once made. As explained, even hardened atheists undergoing an NDE have later confessed they were obliged to recognise that this Power is God.

And, if that is the case, then what happens when the near-death experiencer finds himself banished from the briefly-tasted bliss is nothing less than a divine judgement, as will be further explored in the next chapter.

Chapter 10 -
WEIGHED AND FOUND WANTING

As said before, the saddest part of the near-death experience is being turned away from the unexpected peace, joy and acceptance found flowing from the Beings of light encountered in the afterlife. Yet strangely, most NDErs fail to recognise it for the judgement that it actually is. Rather, they conclude this curtailed taste of bliss was a blessing they expect to be renewed when they finally and irrevocably depart this life.

But is that so? The literature of almost every human culture and that of most religions says otherwise. Indeed, from the earliest times, human beings have been aware that judgement by a higher authority awaits us all at death, a time when we must answer for what we have done in this life.

Ancient Egyptians, for example, believed that at death a person's soul was weighed in a balance by the jackal-faced god of judgement, Anubis, and if found too sinful, was thrown to be eaten by a crocodile.

Indeed, whether we care to admit it or not, there is deeply embedded in our conscience the knowledge that we are answerable for who we are and what we do in this life. The eerie feeling that we will be assessed for good or ill at the end of our life, persists even if we choose to believe that at death we simply cease to exist.

Now, given that every near-death experience ends with banishment from the sphere of ecstasy, we should again ask – though many NDErs don't - what or who makes the judgement that consigns us to such a fate? It is my conviction that this is no less than the judgement the Bible says all humans must undergo at death.

Accordingly, I believe that it is the *'judgement seat of Christ*[51]*,* as specified in the Bible, which the Apostle Paul said even Christian believers must face. Remember, the near-death experience is real; it is a death in progress that is only interrupted by a return to life in the body either by resuscitation or a miraculous recovery as it was in my case. Hence the title of this book, *'Miracle in the Dark'.*

If you fall some 35 feet and land head-first on the rocks you suffer serious injury even if you wear a miner's hat. I attribute my recovery, paralysed and in great pain though I was, to nothing less than a divine intervention that had already deter-mined I was unfit as yet to remain in bliss but needed to be kept alive once back on earth.

To be sent back was my judgement sentence and, if I understand the Bible aright, there will be a similar judgement of staying or going for everyone else, as well. Consider the following:

Hebrews 9:27: *And as it is appointed for men to die once but after this the judgement.*

So, there is judgement coming for everyone, even for born-again, saved Christians:

Romans 14:10: *But why do you judge your brother ... for we shall all stand before the judgement seat of Christ.*

---

[51] 2 Corinthians 5:10

2 Corinthians 5:10*: 'For we must all appear before the judgement seat of Christ that each one may receive the things done in the body, according to what he has done, whether good or bad'.*

Can it be then that what I experienced in my NDE was an excursion to a blessed place only to find myself held to account and found wanting at the judgement seat of Christ? I firmly believe that is so.

Why then, is it not widely recognised among NDErs that their expulsion from the Paradise of love and grace they briefly experienced, is in fact a sentence handed down by the *'judgement seat of Christ'*? Answer: Because until we are born again by God's Spirit and receive Jesus as our Redeemer (that is to be 'saved' in more popular parlance), we have an inbuilt aversion to God, Jesus, and anything the Bible says about Him.

And that instinctive avoidance of believing in and trusting God is why, for many years, I took the totally wrong meaning from my cave venture into the spiritual world beyond. Worse still, I foolishly thought – without any evidence for doing so – that the bliss I briefly tasted would be mine for ever when my earthly life was over. And many millions make the same mistake and come to believe the same untruth.

So, where does one go to find the truth about this important issue? The books and papers written about the near-death experience turn first to neural science and then to psychology. But when physiological and neurological explorations fail to adequately explain what is now increasingly recognised as a spiritual experience, the quest turns to other beliefs.

The out-of-body experience, for example, is interpreted by some as 'astral projection' - the New Age assertion that if practiced enough, a person's soul can float out from the body at their volition to venture far and near - and that this explains what happens in the NDE. But does it?

Other occult explanations for the NDE include spirit travel. As to the NDE's meaning, many believe it points to reincarnation and put their hope for a life after death in that. A later chapter will pit that assertion against the biblical teaching of resurrection.

Returning to my own NDE, one question is: Would I ever have accepted Jesus without this experience? The short answer is: I don't know. However, it undoubtedly opened up my mind to the probability there was a reality beyond the earthy and very limited life I lived. And later when I ran into deep trouble in my life, the memory of a 'life beyond' I once encountered in the dark of a Derbyshire cave, was revived.

Chapter 11 -
A DYING ROBBER'S STORY

There is much confusion about what really happens to us after death. To break through it, let's ask two simple questions:

1) Is it Paradise believers in Jesus go to when they die?

2) Is it Paradise or someplace else near-death experiencers encounter before they are turned back?

To me the story of one man hanging on a cross to die gives the answer. Uncannily, this man really experienced several important NDE features before he actually died, including seeing Jesus as God. What's more, after confessing his sin, repenting and putting his trust in the Lord he was told that that very day he would be with Jesus in Paradise. Fact is, he is the only man in the New Testament to have been given this promise personally. And it is my conviction that the assurance given him is the entry ticket to the realm of bliss for anyone else who is also prepared to repent and trust in Jesus for their salvation.

Dying, this man learned that the One crucified alongside him was both the Messiah (Saviour) and God. Like Jesus, he too was hung on a cross and suffered agony in a drawn-out death. This, for sure, was a 'near-death experience', one that ended for both in real death. This is his story.

You do not know my name. Nor the terrible things I did; robbery, torture, savage beatings and murder among them. You know from the Bible that I was sentenced to death for these crimes. And now you find me nailed to a cross, struggling against awful pain and waiting and wanting to die. A well-deserved end, you think. And I agree. I deserve to die like this for what I have done. For I didn't become a ruthless robber out of desperate need. I did it because I wanted to. Sure, I was brought up in a poor but hard-working family with few prospects. At times, we went without but mostly, there was food on the table.

Actually, crime was a career choice for me. Scraping a living from hard work and little pay had no appeal. I wanted the big money and determined I would do anything to get it. Perhaps you think bad company led me astray? Not so. For I was the one leading others into crime. You see, early in life I was jealous and envious. It was a spirit of always wanting more and hating those who had it. My siblings were different; accepting their lot, they obeyed and helped put bread on the table. Me, I was ashamed my family had to struggle.

So, I put my resentment to work against the better off, children born with a 'silver spoon in their mouth'. I threatened and bullied them, then robbed them and became a terror in the neighbourhood. And, strangely, no-one gave me the beating I richly deserved that might have taught me better. My friends were also bullies and together we became a gang stealing from houses and shops. Then, banished from our homes, we took to the desert, attacking travellers on lonely roads. At first, we merely left our victims badly hurt, but then took to killing them. Safer that way; dead men and women tell no tales.

Eventually of course, we were caught and condemned to death. And it was there on the cross, hanging in agony and being mocked by the crowd that suddenly, I was given new eyes to see the One who, by a miracle, changed my heart in my dying hours. Those hours were between the sixth and ninth hour, as we knew time then, or from noon to 3pm as you know it today. It was then, as scripture records, that *'darkness covered the land'*[52]. And so, night fell in the middle of the day. Thus, the amazing thing that then happened to me was truly a 'miracle in the dark'.

The cross of this very different Man to me stood between mine and that of my fellow robber. We were crying out against anyone and everyone - the judge who sentenced us, the soldiers executing us and the onlookers insulting us. In our mind they were all to blame. And I called down special abuse on Semiramis, the long-dead harlot wife of the demi-god Nimrod, who, it is said, invented crucifixion specifically to enjoy seeing her victims' death agonies.

Amid all this cursing, the Man hung beside me remained calm. Almost peaceful, you might say, despite his agony. When He spoke, it was not to curse or protest. *'Father, forgive them for they know not what they do'* were his surprising words. And that angered my fellow criminal and I. Forgive them! How could He, how could we? So, we took out our anguish on Him. 'How can you stay silent when they're doing this to us?' we roared. My fellow thief went further. *'If you are the Christ, the King of the Jews, God's chosen One, and not an imposter, then save yourself and us. Come down from cross'*[53], he shouted.

---

[52] Matthew 27:45-46
[53] Luke 23:37

It must have been then that I swooned again from pain, just as I had when the nails were first hammered into my wrists and ankles. It was pain beyond pain; for I had been flogged before being crucified. Now I passed out and felt myself leave my body and float upwards above the execution scene. And as I ascended what seemed to be a tunnel, my life of crime was revisited on me. In stark detail each dreadful deed was painfully pointed out. Had mine eyes been with me I would have wept with shame but strangely they seemed absent. As it was, I cringed with remorse, angry at myself for what I had done.

Oh, if only I had lived a better life. And from somewhere way outside myself, yet echoing within me, I sensed a voice saying, 'But you are forgiven'. Forgiven! Impossible I thought. Then the thought came to me that if this Man on his cross could forgive those murdering Him then He could also forgive me. But it was just too hard to believe anyone could forgive me for what I had done.

This is how the inscription in three languages set above Jesus' cross may have looked.

My gaze then turned on the written charge fixed above the quiet Man's head. *'This is Jesus the King of the Jews'* it said in Hebrew, Greek and Latin. Now, I spoke Aramaic, not Hebrew, and knew only a few words in Greek – enough to sell and trade in stolen goods - but little more. Of Latin I knew nothing. Yet somehow, I knew – I don't know how – exactly what each word meant in all three languages. And as I looked on, the words seemed to blaze with fire. It was brought home to me in a flash of inner light, that this Jesus really was a King. Not a conquering warrior as most people hoped He would be. But a King of peace able to forgive his enemies. Enemies that included me. And then in my disembodied state I was turned to see Him in his true state, that of divine glory.

In my vision, as if to prove his royalty and the truth of the flaming proclamation, his body shone as with gold. Gold which turned the cruel thorn circle jammed into his head into a glittering crown. And now I understood. No longer was this Jesus just a victim helplessly agonising toward death, nor a criminal falsely charged with pretending to be Israel's Messiah which is who He actually was. No, He was a King indeed, not just of Israel but also of heaven and all mankind. It came to me, again I know not how, that actually I was now seeing God Himself come as a righteous Man. So righteous He was dying for all the world's sin.

But then horror. I was terrified that this holy Person would also condemn me as others had, for I knew I deserved that. Instead, shockingly, I felt understanding, compassion and forgiveness from Him flood over me. So much so, I temporarily forgot about the nails and the pain. Had I been able, then I would have bowed to Him. As it was, at best, I could only briefly tilt my head downwards. But I knew that somehow, despite the sheer impossibility of such a thing, He had accepted me just as I was, a criminal who richly deserved to die. Astonishingly, feelings of love and the intimation of a life beyond this death flowed from Him and washed over me. Above all, for the first time in my life, I knew I was truly forgiven.

And now a further wonder. Once more I was led to retrace my wicked life. This time, however, the evil things I had done were erased and replaced with good deeds. 'But I can't go back and undo all the wrongs I have done. How can I when I am about to die?' I cried. Then, though hard to believe, I was led to understand that these good works were ones I would do in the life to come and that I could continue in such goodness for ever. But a good life to come after death? I had never dreamt there could be such a thing, especially for one as wicked as I. Punishment in a fiery hell for eternity maybe – it was no more than I deserved. But then as I looked into the Man's eyes, I saw that it was true – through his kindness I could make up for a lifetime of misdeeds. As if to confirm this, a calm peace stole over me.

Then, suddenly, with a sharp jolt of pain I was back in my body on the cross, only to hear my fellow malefactor on his cross again hurling abuse at all around. So, in the light of what I had just seen, but had never known before, I told him, *'Do you not fear God, seeing you are under the same condemnation? And we indeed justly, for we receive the due reward of our deeds but this Man has done nothing wrong'.*[54] There was still more I was shown as I swooned once again. Pain faded to a dull ache, as I sensed the wonder of what it will be when King Jesus comes into the full glory of his kingdom.

---

[54] Luke 23:40-41

Actually, I believe I was flown through time to see what the Prophet Isaiah had seen more than thousand years before my time when he also was carried forward far into the future to see the Lord not being crucified but *'...sitting on a throne, high and lifted up and the train of his robe filled the temple... and one angel cried to another and said the whole earth is full of his glory'* (Isaiah 61-3). So, I turned to Him and said, *'Lord, remember me when you come into your kingdom'*. And He said, *'Assuredly I say to you, today you shall be with Me in Paradise'*.[55]

Paradise! What a word! You mean Lord, that before the sun goes down you and I are going be in the Garden of God, the Eden of everything that is good, the place that men and women on earth have not known since you drove them out and closed the gate on it long, long ago? And He nodded his head. What, you might ask, as I did in my mind, is the essence of this Paradise that the Lord told me I would enter with Him? And it came to me that just as God had walked and talked in the garden with Adam and Eve before they sinned, so I would be able to talk with and be with this Jesus forever. For wherever He is, this is Paradise for sure.

Now, what became clear to me as I hung waiting for my inevitable death, and no longer fearing it, was that I was fully forgiven just because Jesus the Messiah King had suffered alongside me to bear the punishment for me. For my own execution, even if repeated a thousand times, could not even begin to discharge my awful debt of sin. But this holy man Jesus, through his death, removed it totally. And then, hours before I also reached my end, the

---

[55] Luke 23:42-43

scene changed again. An earthquake struck and the King I had come to love, died crying out, *'It is finished'*. [56] And I saw Him give up his life, having first commended his spirit into the hands of his Father above.

Now, He was parted from me and my pain returned strongly. However, I found I could place myself partly beyond it by resting in his promise that I should soon be with Him in glory. And when, finally, they came to break my legs, so that I died before Passover began, death came to me at last. But that wasn't the end of me. If I am allowed to speak beyond the reach of time, I would say that I awoke to find myself indeed in Paradise. You see, there was no judgement, no hearing before a court, to decide whether I was worthy or not to enter this abode of bliss. I simply entered in and found I was allowed to stay.

Why? Because that judgement had already taken place when both the Lord and I were dying on the cross. Because it was He, not me, who died to fully pay for my sins.

---

[56] John 19:30

Chapter 12 -
WHAT THE ANCIENTS KNEW

Thousands of years ago, our predecessors seem to have known more of what really happens in the lead up to, and experience of death, than the supposedly knowledgeable neurological experts of our pre-dominantly secular, western world today. What's puzzling, is why their conclusions about this profound process, which are clearly based, not only on personal experience, but also on the perceived and received wisdom of their time, are largely ignored today in the quest to understand NDE.

The truth is that today's much-vaunted science, which both for philosophic and pragmatic reasons in our now post-Christian western world, is held to be the answer to understanding all things, cannot provide a satisfactory explanation for the beautiful, sometimes frightening, near-death experience.

And this, for the simple reason that science at heart, is materialistic. It cannot envisage nor admit of anything that is not composed of matter or energy. Anything that is spiritual, i.e., non-material, and not a product of energy, is left out of the equation. But, like it or not, there is another dimension to our apparent three or four-dimensional world. Beyond length, breadth, depth and time, there is another realm, a spiritual world that, no matter how dimly glimpsed, is sensed by every person.

To the ancients, this 'other world' was very real. Indeed, it was not until the 1700s and the so-called 'Enlightenment' – a misnomer if there ever was one – that science threw out the 'top storey' of spiritual, heavenly and 'other-worldly' experience to concentrate on that which could be physically seen, heard, felt and measured on 'the lower floor'.

Participants in the Enlightenment, also known as the Age of Reason, thought they were illuminating human intellect and culture after the 'dark' Middle Ages. They believed increased knowledge, applying reason, and adherence to scientific method would bring about greater progress and happiness.

The world, they said, was rational and beneficent; nature, including humanity, was essentially good and that 'enlightened' people had the potential to improve themselves and their environment. The prospect held out, was the making of a 'far better world'. The reality, as it worked out, was far more the nightmare George Orwell described in his book, *'Brave New World'*, as a mere glance at the history of the last 300-plus years clearly shows.

Far from 'enlightening our days', science *falsely so called*'[57] has brought us worldwide wars, rampant slavery, ruthless exploitation, the unproven doctrine of evolution (giving rise to both Communism and Fascism), destruction of morality and unbelief in God the Creator and Saviour of mankind. To my mind, the looked-for scientific 'progress', far from creating a philosophic paradise is actually epitomised more by invention of the guillotine and hydrogen bomb, the torture and murder of massacred millions and the supposed 'death of God'.

Worse still, the wisdom of the ancients, their understanding of the universe and the way things really are, has been dumped.

---

1 Timothy 6:20

For example, prior to the birth of Christ it was a universal truth held across all cultures that mankind had 'begun again' as descendants of Noah's three sons after the Flood. In fact, there are very few human remains and few recognised and dateable pieces of archaeological evidence that have been found to have preceded the Flood, which is said to have occurred around 3,000 BC.

Today, of course, science, archaeology, geology and accepted history all poo-poo the deluge as a myth. Yet no alternative, meaningful explanation, of how mankind quickly spread around the globe a few thousand years ago after a global flood, can be made that does not begin with Noah's family, and has the mountains of Ararat in present day Turkey as its starting point.

Furthermore, all river deltas can be traced back to beginnings that coincide in occurring about 4,600 years ago. However, it was the Greek philosopher Plato who first introduced the misleading doctrine that it is the human soul that survives death and goes to heaven or hell, depending upon its behaviour in this life. This in defiance of Psalm 22: 29, which says:

> *... all they that go down to the dust (i.e., die) shall bow before Him (i.e., the Messiah Lord) and none can keep alive his own soul.*

It seems Plato knew little or nothing of the human spirit since he does not mention it or treats the words 'spirit' and 'soul' as synonymous, i.e., meaning the same thing. In doing so, he told of the very real NDE of a warrior of his time:

Er, a warrior bold, was son of Armenious, by race a Pamphylian. Slain in battle, he was found intact when the

corpses were taken up on the tenth day already decayed. He was brought home and at his funeral, revived on his funeral pyre and related what he had seen in the world beyond. He said that when his 'soul went forth from his body,' he journeyed with a great company that came to a mysterious region where there were two openings (or caves) side by side in the Earth, and above and over against them in the heaven two others. He said 'judges' sat between bidding the 'righteous' to journey to the right and upward to heaven and the 'unjust' to take the road to the left and downward to another place. When Er himself drew near, these judges told him that he must be the messenger to humanity to tell them of this other world, and charged him to 'give ear and to observe everything in the place'. (Rep. X,614 b,c,d).

Er's account is one thing; what Plato made of it, another. Undoubtedly, Er had a real near-death experience but Plato embellished it and turned it into a collective cosmology that has warped mankind's thinking ever since. In particular, his assertions of an 'immortal soul' and punishment and reward in an afterlife so strongly misshaped some Christian ideas that even now, his pagan thoughts are preferred to the plain statements of scripture that teach the opposite to them. To this day, such false beliefs are set in concrete by some major churches, as doctrines that must be believed and obeyed. For example, it is from Plato that almost every religion, parts of Christianity included, gets the false notion that after death, the soul lives on in some form or another. But if that's true, then Jesus is a liar and so are his apostles and the Old Testament prophets.

The Prophet Ezekiel twice wrote: '*The soul that sinneth it shall die*' (Ezekiel 18:4, 20). And that includes your soul and mine, for we have all sinned. Jesus Christ warned his apostles, *'Fear not those that can kill the body but are not able to kill the soul, but rather fear Him which is able to destroy both soul and body in hell* (i.e., the grave) (Matt.10:28). The 'Him' of course, is God.

Psalm 89:48 asks a rhetorical question: *'What man is he that liveth and shall not see death? Shall he deliver his soul from the hand (i.e., the power) of the grave?'* Obviously not, is the answer. Jesus Himself warned: *'What shall it profit a man if he shall gain the whole world and lose his own soul?'* (Mark 8:36).

Clearly then, souls can be lost; that is, they can die and be lost to life.

Chapter 13 -
THE SOUL'S DEATH

So, far from living on, because it is supposedly immortal, our soul actually dies. Even the soul of Jesus - God who became man - died and with his body lay dead in the grave - and we have the authority of the Apostle Peter for that, saying that after his crucifixion '*... his soul was not left in hell (Greek Hades, the place of the dead; i.e., the grave) neither did his flesh see corruption'*.

Fact is, that for a measurable period of time, the soul of Jesus did lie dead with his body in the tomb. However, God didn't leave it there but resurrected Jesus as a whole human being, body, soul and spirit, to new life. And his promise is that those who trust and obey Him, eventually can be resurrected too.

Now the soul is the essence of our personality; thus, when it dies, we die with it. For without a soul, we have no earthly natural self-consciousness. Thus, when God pronounced death upon Adam, the man He had created, for his sin of eating the forbidden fruit, He did not say, 'Your immortal soul will live on'. Rather he told Adam that he would die and return to the ground from which he was taken: '*For dust thou art and unto dust thou shalt return*' (Genesis 3:19). In other words, you will surely die.

So, what actually remains of a once live human being when they die? The short answer for many is nothing. The body rots in the ground, the soul dies with it and apparently all consciousness ceases. But what about the spirit? I hear you ask.

Good question. Ecclesiastes 12:7 sums up the state of our death and also answers the query, saying, '*Then shall the dust return to the earth as it was: and the **spirit** shall return to God who gave it*'.

And so, it is to the spirit, not the soul, that we must look, if we are to grasp the huge significance of the near-death experience and the message it has for all who will believe it.

Meantime, let's say a prayer for all those who have been taught by churches and teachers of pagan beliefs to hold that at death, everybody's soul flies straight to heaven to live in happiness. It doesn't, and they have been deceived. If Jesus is to be believed, the soul dies with the body in the ground - or is consumed in the crematorium incinerator if one can't afford a grave.

Death is both inevitable and irrevocable for everybody, unless they believe in Jesus as Lord and Saviour, and thus qualify for later bodily resurrection to life in a new and better world on earth. Read about that in John 11:25-26 (NKJV):

> *Jesus said to her (Martha) I am the resurrection and the life. He who believes in Me though he may die yet shall he live. And whoever dies and believes in Me shall never die. Do you believe this?*

But what about 2 Corinthians 5:8-9, where the Apostle Paul speaks of being '*willing to be absent from the body and present with the Lord*' with the subsequent condition that we need to be '*accepted by Him*'?

Yes, this verse does teach there is one sense in which we can be with the Lord though dead. It is that our spirit returns to Him, since He was the one who gave it. In verse 9 Paul says he makes it always his aim to be '*well pleasing to Him,*' clearly inferring this is the necessary qualification to, at death, go to be '*present with the Lord*'. And here's the shocker. In verse 10 the apostle insists that *'we must appear before the judgement seat of Christ'* to be assessed *'for the things done in the body'*.

This does not mean we as believers will be hauled over the coals for every sin we have committed – as, for believers, such sins are already forgiven and forgotten by God, washed away by the blood of Jesus shed on the cross. No, it is what we have done for God since we came to know Jesus as our Saviour, that is in question. For the *'judgement seat of Christ'* is far more about rewarding faithful and obedient believers than punishing them.

Getting back to Plato, he used various elements of Er's incredible and embellished NDE story to fashion a new doctrine of 'ultimate justice' that redefines what happens at death and afterwards, even though his view defies established truth and experience. His aim was to combat the then popular Greek idea that death was the same for all, no matter whether they had done good or bad during their life. In this view, the dead simply went to the shadowy land of Hades where they were neither punished nor rewarded but soon forgotten.

He was, of course, drawing on pagan traditions derived from Egypt and Babylon. The idea that man has an 'immortal soul' that upon death is judged and sent either to heaven or to a fiery hell, is an ancient belief. It began in the Garden of Eden, with Satan's lie to Eve that in eating the forbidden fruit, *'thou surely shall not die'* (Genesis 3:4). But when Cain slew Abel, it became all too clear that, although once created in the image of God, man could indeed die.

Faced with this evidence and the reproach of Adam and Eve for having deceived them, Satan came up with a new explanation. Yes, the body had died but the soul lived on, he argued – and with few exceptions, mankind has believed that lie ever since.

Major Christian denominations teach, as do Islam and Hinduism, that there is an afterlife in which the dead (that is, their souls) are sent either to heaven or hell. Even the most animistic peoples believe the souls of their ancestors are alive (hence supposedly immortal) and communicate with them, and that there is punishment or reward for them beyond the grave. Yet, all this defies and contradicts what the Bible actually says about immortality, which is the power to **not** die but have the potential to live on for ever.

Unfortunately, for all those who hold that the soul lives on after death and goes to heaven, there is bad news in 1 Timothy 6:11-16, in the King James Bible. Here the Apostle Paul urges his disciple Timothy to *'fight the good of faith'*, by *'following after righteousness, godliness, faith, love, patience and meekness'* until *'the **appearing** of our Lord Jesus Christ'*. He then goes on to say:

> *Which in his times He shall shew, who is the blessed and only Potentate, the King of kings and Lord of lords, **who only hath immortality,** dwelling light **which no man can approach unto, whom no man hath seen, nor can see ...**

Here the Apostle Paul, speaking with God-given authority, pronounces that at present only one man has immortality. That is to say, only one man, Christ Jesus, has an immortal soul. The rest of us do not. What's more this truth suggests that the light Christ Jesus dwells in is the one glimpsed, but not grasped to hold on to, in the near-death experience.

Interestingly, Plato in the legend of *Phaestus*, describes 'the flight of the immortal soul (sic) towards an incredible vision of pure celestial being' as drawing near to light. He holds that the very purpose of philosophy, indeed the goal of man's life, is to remember that 'primal vision of pure, powerful Light'.

For Plato, history's main proponent of reincarnation philosophy, this vision is only experienced 'between lives', that is, in the supposed 'pilgrimage between death and (re)birth'. In *Phaestus* he pictures the soul, drawn out by 'love and beauty' and carried as on a chariot pulled by eager steeds upward, to join a magnificent circular parade of souls (forming the Milky Way). All parade around this cosmic circle, each following his own god and straining 'for a view of the pure 'Being' in the centre'.

As said, Plato has profound influence on human thinking. His teaching of reincarnation is the 'default position' adopted by most people seeking to understand what lies beyond death. And there is truth, albeit greatly distorted, in some of what he has to say.

For example, there really is a great Being of pure light we should be looking for (Titus 2:13). His name is Christ Jesus, but the problem is that, in our present earthly life, we cannot see Him, except by the eye of faith. As 1 Timothy 6:16 says, at present this immortal Being cannot be seen. However, He can be 'sensed' through the spirit which, I believe, is temporarily *'quickened'* or made alive in the near-death experience in order to do so.

Nevertheless, the great hope for mankind right now is the biblical promise of Christ's imminent *'appearing'*, not only to saints but also to the world. This will occur in what Paul calls the *'Day of Christ'* (1 Corinthians 1:8, Philippians 1:10, 2:16) when, from heaven, the Lord Jesus will fully display Himself, not only as the only immortal man, but importantly, as the great God who is the rightful ruler of men, heaven, earth and the universe. (See also Titus 2:13 and 2 Timothy 4:1). In other words, He will not only make Himself seen by all but also take control and hugely change the world for the better.

In contrast, while, as we have seen, Plato knew of the near-death experience, he interpreted it in the light of his non-scriptural, pagan theory of reincarnation, thus giving rise to belief in gods many, rather than the One True God.

A very different understanding of the NDE phenomenon comes from the Apostle Paul, Charles Wesley and others who, while in this life, and without passing from death to any re-birth, nevertheless experienced a 'quickening' or 'awakening'. Their testimony is that this experience came in an encounter with the 'One and only true God' who was and is and always will be a Being of great light, and who took it upon Himself to 'awaken' them.

Subsequently, 'awakening' was the very term used to describe the deeply moving experience that brought millions to know Christ as their Saviour on both sides of the Atlantic in the 18th-century Wesley-Whitefield revivals. And such quickening or awakening, far from being a religious performance or ceremony, was a real, non-contrived, spontaneous occurrence, very much like an NDE. A later chapter further examines such awakening, or quickening as it is also known in scripture, and explores its connection with the Being(s) of light encountered in near-death experiences.

In the meantime, let me say that without doubt NDE experiences have occurred throughout history and provoked deep thought about death and what follows after it. What then is their essential purpose?

Chapter 14 - AN ATHEIST FINDS GOD

If NDE were an infectious disease then one would have to describe it as an epidemic, because the number of people undergoing or being affected by it is far greater than you might think. For example, I recently asked a group of New Zealanders at a meeting I attended, if they had had a near-death experience, and more than half put their hands up.

A Gallup poll in the United States found that nearly 12 million people claimed experience of life beyond the grave, while in Britain, according to a Mori poll, seven people out of ten believed that NDEs really do happen, and that they constitute true evidence of an afterlife. Surveys show that when asked to describe what happened NDEers show an amazing similarity in their accounts.

They nearly all experience a **tunnel**, a **rushing sound, a brilliant light, a feeling of ecstasy** and **being told it is not yet time to die**. Also frequent are: the **out-of-the-body experience** in which a person appears to observe his body from above, often watching medics trying frantically to revive his corpse; **an instantaneous review of a person's whole life**; and sometimes **seeing dead friends** and family.

One woman said she met a brother she did not know she had. Her father told her later: 'You did have a brother. I am the only one alive who knew about him'. Others, particularly atheists, report seeing God or Jesus, for them a life shattering experience, and many experience a huge expansion of knowledge.

A 'typical NDE' case that has most of the elements was reported in the article, *'Can There Be Life After Life? Ask the Atheist!'* by prominent British journalist Gerry Loughran, (Letter From London, March 18, 2001). It is the near-death encounter of Jack Foreman, a US naval technician who was 'cooked' by a radiation leak and had major surgery for a large hole in his diaphragm.

Several days later, he appeared to die. 'I could look down on my whole body,' he later reported. 'One medic was applying electric paddles to my chest to shock me back and shouting "Breathe, you son-of-a-bitch, breathe". They stabbed needles into his lungs to extract fluid and injected adrenaline direct into the heart.

Foreman says he saw his entire life pass in seconds: from being in the womb, through his christening to an embarrassing incident as a small boy when he soiled his pants. He heard a loud rushing noise and appeared to be speeding through a dark tunnel with a light of unbearable brightness at the end.

This light took human form and he received a message, though not in audible words, 'You must go back'. The tunnel experience then happened in reverse. Because of its radioactive status, Foreman's body had been taken to a cleaning room. He had a feeling that he re-entered painfully through his toes and when he spoke, the medics who by then considered him dead were totally shocked.

Remarkably, the majority of those who have near-death experiences report they had intense feelings of joy and comfort. Indeed, a statistician calculated that 69 per cent of thousands of cases he investigated, said the heart of their experience was encountering a feeling of overwhelming love.

Stunningly, when a researcher categorised his NDE subjects according to their beliefs (i.e., Christian, Religious but non-Christian, Non-religious, New Age, etc.) he found that 100 per cent of those calling themselves 'atheist' had experienced 'tremendous ecstasy' while 63 per cent underwent a life review experience.

Now when one of the most ardent of atheists affirms the reality of the near-death experience and goes so far as to report that 'he had seen God', then it's time for medicine and science to sit up and take notice. Persuasive philosopher A. J. Ayer, shook the British academic establishment to its core when, after years of having publicly maintained 'there is no God, no afterlife,' he changed his mind as a result of a personal NDE.

As a fierce atheistic student, he debated with some of the greatest minds in the country, including the formidable Jesuit Fr. Martin d'Arcy who described Ayer when he was only 21 as 'the most dangerous man in Oxford University'. Educated at Eton, Oxford after serving in the (Welsh) Guards, Ayer became a popularly-known philosopher by appearing on the BBC radio programme, the *'Brains Trust'*.

Despite his highly charged intellect, Ayer's account of his NDE is surprisingly similar to that of others. His brush with death came in 1988 when his heart stopped while he choked on smoked salmon, and he confessed that for four minutes he was in 'another place'. He wrote of seeing 'a red light for governing the universe' and crossing some barrier 'like the River Styx'. 'It weakened my conviction that death would be the end of me, though I continue to hope it will be.'

Ayer's experience put NDE back on the front pages of British newspapers and reopened the debate as to what it meant. Many of his friends felt Ayer's published account reflected his philosophic urge to embellish and tease. He was 'playing to the crowd'. None, however, denied Ayer's claim to have had an extraordinary experience while his heart was stopped. And a year later, his wife said, 'Freddie has been so much nicer since he died'. What his friends questioned was whether his NDE account was the entire truth.

For, years later the surgeon who had attended Ayer broke a long silence. He told an author who wrote a play about the affair: 'Ayer told me he saw the Supreme Being'. There was no further elucidation. The physician said simply that when Ayer recovered, 'he told me he saw the Supreme Being'.

His friends were astounded. Ayer had admitted there was a God! Was this another joke? If not, why did he withhold it from his story? Was it that he could not face the possibility that he had built a glittering career on a false premise? The famed philosopher had seen and heard things he had spent a lifetime denying.

But Ayer is not the only person to have 'seen the light' and been radically changed by it. A statistical survey of atheists who underwent a near-death experience revealed that:

- One hundred percent of them reported having a life review, more than any other category of those experiencing NDE.

- Seventy five percent reported experiencing overwhelming love, again more than any other category.

- Concerning the NDE aspect of seeing God, 75 percent of atheists asserted they saw a Divine Being.

- Fifty percent reported feeling 'extreme ecstasy'.

- Sixty three percent of atheists asserted they received 'unlimited knowledge' during and as a consequence of their NDE, more than experiencers in any other category.
- Most striking of all, 50 percent of atheists interviewed after having had an NDE reported that they had seen Jesus.

All this sends a clear message to atheists, agnostics, sceptics and other doubters. If you want to persist in believing there is no God, then better make sure you don't have a near-death experience. One former atheist, Paul Ammon, whose story is featured in Penny Sartori and Kelly Walsh's book, *'The Transformative Power of Near-death Experiences'*, had three NDEs before finally coming to the 'amazing realisation that there is a loving God'.

Ammon unknowingly developed a blood clot which later broke free and went to his lungs when he was high in the mountains of New Mexico with his dog Sheba. He fell into a coma that lasted four days and would have died had not the dog run for help. He was taken to hospital in a critical condition with multiple complications and was told he was dying. Instead, he felt incredible love, blissful timelessness and, despite his condition, no pain. Then Ammon 'left his body' and gives this account of what happened next:

> I found myself in a place of darkness, a series of multiple dimensions on what seemed to be the edge of infinity. Star-like objects moved all around me, forming a vortex with a white, bright core. I had a very strong sense of being cared for. Something told me not to go with the other lights into the core, which seemed to be the gate to

heaven. I was connected to everything and everything was connected to me. I was one with the other spirits and could communicate with them. Not so much through words, but through emotions. Emotions that were louder than words mixed with all my other senses. I wanted so badly to join the spirits in light but understood I could not. I was returned to my physical body. My doctors had speculated that if I didn't die, I'd most likely be a vegetable on a dialysis machine. I beat the odds and awakened back in my body in the intensive care unit. It felt like hell compared to where I had been. Having been an atheist most of my life, I was filled with shame and pain over the way I had lived and the things I had believed. After 13 years and two more NDEs, I came to the amazing realisation that there is a loving God.

Chapter 15 - THE BLACKNESS OF DARKNESS

It was black in the cave and even darker in my soul. Jude in the Bible (Jude 13) calls this the *'blackness of darkness for ever'*, which is reserved, he says, for ungodly unbelievers who *'separate themselves (from God and are) sensual having not the Spirit'*. You see, knowing we have a spirit that can feel and know is vital to understanding what the near-death, out-of-body experience is really about. For, in all that has been written and said about the NDE – and that's heaps – few answer a crucial question.

That question is: What part of each one of us is it that leaves the body and can journey into the next world to experience another reality? What faculty of ours knows what we experience there? The answer according to psychiatrists is that it is our subconscious mind. Those less 'scientific' assert it is the soul which we are told is our mind, will and emotions. But the biblical truth is that when our body dies the soul ceases to function. Thus, speaking of death, Ecclesiastes 12:7 says: *Then shall the dust return to the earth as it was; and the spirit shall return to God who gave it.*

In other words, when a person dies, his or her spirit goes back to God, the body returns to dust and the soul of that person no longer exists. Why? Because the first man, Adam, only became a *'living soul'* when God the Creator, who is Spirit, breathed his own breath into Adam's nostrils *'and man became a living soul'*[58]. Consequently, when we die our soul, which is our life, dies because when the spirit leaves to return to God we die and are no longer a soul.

That's why Jesus challenges us all when He speaks of taking up the cross and following Him, then says (Matthew 16:25):

> *Whoever wants to save his life (lit. soul) shall lose it but whoever loses his life for my sake shall find it. What is a man profited if he gained the whole world and lose his own soul? Or what shall a man give in exchange for his soul?*

So, the soul is our life; the two terms are interchangeable. And, in a genuine near-death experience the soul during that time ceases to exist. And medical experts confirm that brain dead patients on the operating table nevertheless can vividly report detailed accounts of their excursion into the 'other realm'.

Evidently their soul did not accompany them on the journey, nor did it see, hear, feel or sense at that time because it was dead. So, what did? The answer is one's spirit. You and I are tripartite beings composed of body soul and spirit even if we don't know it. (For evidence see 1 Thessalonians 5:23 in the Bible).

Further proof that at death the soul dies also is found in 1 Kings 17:17-22 recounting the near or actual death experience of the widow's son who revived at the prayer of the prophet Elijah. Verse 22 says: *'And the Lord heard the voice of Elijah and the soul of the child came into him again and he revived'.*

---

[58] Genesis 2:7

Now here's a stunning proof of that fact that our spirit can see, feel, sense, hear and perceive when the rest of our being is dead. As you now know my own near-death took place in the pitch-dark blackness of a cave deep underground. Consequently, nothing I saw was seen with my natural sight.

Nevertheless, what I did see were two shades of blackness (that is, first the dark of the cave and then, secondly, as it was revealed to me, the blackness in my own soul). Then I saw a kindly light sourced from Beings in white who exuded such love and compassion the like of which I have never experienced otherwise in my life.

This, when I all but died, yet remarkably, lived to tell the tale. Let me state clearly that my journey to the brink of the afterlife has been the most striking experience in my life to date. Now late in life, it still means more to me than almost anything else. Why? Because I am convinced I will soon undergo a similar journey again, but this time, I hope, with a much happier, everlasting outcome.

Chapter 16 -
OUT OF BODY, INTO THE BIBLE?

Near-death and out-of-body experiencers return to their earthly life variously saying they met God Himself, Jesus Christ or other 'Beings' living in that brilliant light only encountered on the 'other side'. And I am sure they did indeed glimpse such holy persons. What's more, they were also assessed – judged if you like - and were overwhelmed with sadness when told they must return to their earthly life in the body. The truth must be faced that neither I nor any other NDEr who has returned to tell their tale, was found good enough to be allowed to stay on in the bliss we so briefly tasted.

So, what was really happening to myself and other NDErs? Most would agree that we had entered another world, a place of spiritual bliss and absolute rightness where we ourselves also felt we could be right or be made right. But then we were turned away. Why? I again suggest it was because we were assessed as not fit at that time to remain in that blessed place, even though we instinctively recognised it as our forever home. So, is what happened to us what the Bible calls, *the judgement seat of Christ*?

As already argued, I believe it is, because the importance of this great event is set out in detail by the Apostle Paul who, he tells us in his writings, underwent not one but frequent near-death and out-of-the body experiences. So, did Paul himself appear at the judgement seat of Christ during his NDEs? My conviction is that he did. How else could he describe in such detail what that experience is?

History records he was whipped five times within an inch of his life (each time with 39 strokes), beaten three times with rods, shipwrecked, cast into the ocean and also stoned. He also experienced trances. All of which would likely make him the most experienced NDEr of all history and certainly the man qualified beyond any other to tell us what the experience really is. And this he does in his epistles (letters) in the Bible.

But what have Bible verses to do with an out-of-body experience, you ask? Answer: A great deal because in 2 Corinthians chapter five, no less than nine verses talk about 'in- or out-of-the-body' events. Then in verse 10 (AMP), Paul says:

> *For we must all appear and be revealed as we are before the judgement seat of Christ so that each may receive [his pay] according to what he has done in the body, whether good or evil [considering what his purpose and motive may have been, and what he has achieved, been busy with, and given himself and his attention to accomplishing].*

There can be no denying that being revealed as we are and having our life to date assessed as it is re-reeled before us, has been present in nearly all out-of-body, near-death experiences. What's more, most NDEers know we were also shown what our life could have been like, had we yielded to the good and right and not the bad impulses that assail us.

This is judgement indeed, but merciful judgement, in that we were given a taste of what living in heaven could be like, then sent back to our body with the opportunity to find God through Jesus Christ as our Saviour while still on earth and, importantly, before our time here runs out. Furthermore, according to the Bible such judgement occurs in a person's life at death or, as some of us have learned, at near death. Hebrews 9:27-28 explains:

> *And just as it is appointed for [all] men once to die, and after that the [certain] judgement. Even so it is that Christ, having been offered to take upon Himself and bear as a burden the sins of many once and once for all, will appear a second time, not to carry any burden of sin, nor to deal with sin, but to bring to full salvation those who are [eagerly, constantly and patiently waiting for and expecting Him]. (AMP).*

As said, nine verses in 2 Corinthians 5 give a detailed presentation of this judgement which occurs at our actual or near death. Paul insists such judgement will come to each and every one of us and explains that the verdict rendered will either be reward (for saved believers that is) or exile from Paradise for those who have rejected Jesus as Saviour and Lord. And in my view, Paul's testimony and other Bible passages on the subject comprise the only plausible statements revealing the purpose of the NDE phenomenon.

To explain further, 2 Corinthians 5:1, cited below, tells a tale, not of two cities, but of two bodies (more on this later). The first is our present earthly body which Paul infers will be destroyed or dissolved, and a second body which we as believers have from God; that is, *'a house not made with hands, eternal in the heavens'.*[59] Now surely, when writing in verse 2 (KJV), the Apostle Paul speaks for us all, especially NDErs, when he says:

---

[59] 2 Corinthians 5:1

For in this [body] we groan earnestly desiring to be clothed upon with our house which is from heaven... For we that are in this tabernacle [body] do groan, being burdened, not that we would be unclothed [i.e., naked] but clothed upon that mortality [our dying] might be swallowed up of life.

There are no NDErs who do not long to know again the peace and joy they briefly felt in their out-of-body experience. Many, myself included, strongly felt this was and should be our forever home. Paul speaks for many when he says: '...*we are willing rather to be absent from the body and to be present with the Lord.*'

But you guessed it, there are certain requirements to be met before we can be confident of going to this blessed place when we finally depart this life for good. First, and most important we must come to know Jesus Christ as Saviour. We need to realise only He can save us from our sin and freely forgive us. Secondly, we must then obey Him as Lord; that is, we must do what He tells us to do. When we so obey, we find that God has given us the Holy Spirit as a guarantee [or down payment] on his promise to one day cause us to be at home with Him (verse 5).

So, 'out of body' people should have no difficulty in understanding what the Apostle says in verse 6 that '...*while we are at home in the (earthly) body we are absent from the Lord*'.

Chapter 17 -
ENTER THE FAKERS

There is, of course, the faked, dubious or over-imagined alleged near-death experience that really isn't a genuine spiritual NDE at all. As witness this American newspaper headline: '**Heaven faker boy and mum evicted by dad'.** The story read:

An Ohio mother is asking the public to pray for her family after she and her quadriplegic son – who's best known for fabricating a story about going to Heaven - were evicted from their home by her ex-husband. Beth Malarkey and her 24-year-old son, Alex, were ordered to leave their home in Huntsville, Ohio, located roughly 40 miles northwest of Columbus, following a hearing on Oct. 1. Alex was left a quadriplegic following a 2004 car accident, which was made famous in the 2010 bestseller, '*The Boy Who Came Back from Heaven'.* In 2015, Malarkey admitted[60] the tale was a total fabrication made up by his father, Kevin Malarkey, who has since divorced Beth and continues to receive 100% of the royalties from the book. He also maintains that Alex's story was true. Following the scandal, Alex sent a letter to LifeWay Christian Stores and other faith-based booksellers,

---

[60] https://www.christianpost.com/news/boy-who-came-back-from-heaven-publisher-retailer-warned-story-was-a-lie-continued-to-sell-despite-concerns-from-mother-christian-leaders-132775/

explaining why he initially went along with his father's fabrications.[61] 'I said I went to Heaven because I thought it would get me attention,' Malarkey wrote. 'When I made the claims that I did, I had never read the Bible. People have profited from lies, and continue to. They should read the Bible, which is enough. The Bible is the only source of truth. Anything written by man cannot be infallible'. Now, after Kevin Malarkey filed an eviction notice against his ex-wife and son, Beth and Alex have moved into a home in nearby Bellefontaine with some help from the Logan County Board of Developmental Disabilities.

Of course, among the thousands of reported NDE cases there will be those that have been, to some extent, made up or have been augmented by overworked imaginations. Trapped in our own limited concepts, it is all too easy to read some of them into what is otherwise a real and true near-death experience.

But, let it be said, the overwhelming majority of those reporting their NDE encounters with the 'world beyond' are not exaggerating nor given to wild fantasies. Their testimony is sober and true.

---

[61] https://www.christianpost.com/news/boy-who-claimed-he-visited-heaven-reads-bible-and-recants-story-lifeway-to-pull-book-from-stores-132646/

Chapter 18 -
WHICH PART OF YOU
LIVES ON AFTER DEATH?

If the Bible is believed, then not only is it possible for fleshly human beings like you and I to meet Christ and other spirit beings in the afterlife, but it is actually achievable. One verse among several others on the topic explains how. In Hebrews 12:22 in the Amplified Bible, we read:

> *But ... you have come Mount Zion, even to the city of the Living God, the heavenly Jerusalem, and to countless multitudes of angels in festive gathering. And to the church (assembly) of the Firstborn who are registered (as citizens) in heaven, and to the God who is Judge of all, and to **the spirits of the righteous** (the redeemed in heaven) who have been made perfect.*

Unpacking this passage to see what light it sheds on the near-death experience, we see that it's talking about a heavenly place or experience not an earthly one. It's also clear that the fellow beings which believers will encounter in this heavenly *'city of God'*, are spirits and not souls. What's more, it is believers still in their bodies on earth, that are being told they have already come to 'Mount Zion', that place of spirits in the afterlife.

The distinct citing of spirits, not souls, is important because so many believe it is their soul that will go to heaven and live on in the afterlife, and not their spirit. Others confuse soul and spirit thinking they are the same. However, the Bible truth is that at death both our body and our soul die and only the spirit remains alive to face ultimate determination at the afore-mentioned judgement seat of Christ. Thus, Jesus told his disciples (Matthew 10:28 and Mark 10:36 (AMP):

> *... do not be afraid of those that can kill the body but cannot kill the soul. Rather be afraid of him who can destroy both body and soul in hell (Gehenna). And:*

> *For what does it profit a man to gain the whole world and forfeit his life (i.e., soul) [in the eternal kingdom of God.*

To explain: Gehenna in Jesus' time was the ever-rotting, ever-burning rubbish tip of Jerusalem. Called the 'Valley of Hinnom' it was where children were once sacrificed by fire to Molech. It became a symbol for judgement [62] and later for final punishment. A place of unquenchable or eternal fire, it is pictured in Revelation as a lake of burning fire and brimstone which will be the fate of the unsaved.[63]

By the by, I personally do not think God will torment the unsaved forever in a burning hell; it would be against His character to do so. However, I do believe He may destroy the bodies and souls of those who refuse His offer of salvation in such a place of everlasting fire.

The main point to take, however, is that it is not the souls of men made righteous with God that will be found in heaven

---

[62] Jeremiah 7:31-32
[63] IVF New Bible Dictionary, Mark 9:43, Matthew 18:8, Revelation 20:10.

but their spirits. An alternative view asserts that both the spirit and soul of believers go to heaven in the afterlife. However, it is hard to find scriptural support for this conclusion.

An important consideration is that Jesus said: *'It is the Spirit who gives life, the 'flesh profits nothing. The words that I speak to you are spirit and they are life'.*[64]And since the Spirit is Christ Himself, it becomes clear that becoming a Christian means living in the Spirit of Christ, not one's soul, and being changed progressively to become like Christ. One commentator puts it well:

> The soul can be described as your personality, your thoughts, your attitudes and what makes you unique. Perhaps this is why we use words like spirit and soul interchangeably because we cannot see either one, yet we understand that we possess something that makes up who we are as a person.
>
> Our spirit is our life force. It is the part of us that was born again when we put our faith in Jesus. The default sin nature was taken out and we were given a new spirit that is identical to Jesus (Romans 6:6-7; I John 4:17). The believer's spirit is the part that has been sanctified, sealed and redeemed (Ephesians 1:13-14; Romans 8:15-17). The spirit you have now is the same spirit you will have for all eternity, it is perfect (Romans 8; Hebrews 10:10; 10:14).

In Hebrews 4:12, we are told that the Word of God is powerful because it is able to discern the difference between the soul and spirit, even though many people understand them to be the same thing. Why is the difference so important? Answer:

---

[64] John 6:63

Because it is in our spirit, not our soul, we will live in the afterlife, in eternity, if you will. Meantime our task is to learn to live in the spirit in our present earth-bound life and bring our soul (our own mind, will and emotions) into subjection to it.

That's why Jesus said: *'God is Spirit and those who worship Him must worship Him in spirit and in truth'.*[65] **It's also why Paul insists that:**

If you live according to the flesh (that is one's ordinary human nature) you will die, but if by the Spirit you put to death the deeds of the body you will live. For as many as are led by the Spirit of God, these are the sons of God.[66]

And again, it's why Jesus said: 'It is the Spirit who gives life; the flesh profits nothing.'

The soul, which essentially is me and how I think and feel, has no life of its own. For true life, eternal life, is derived from my spirit, provided that is, that my spirit has been brought back from being 'dead', i.e., inactive, by the infusion of God's Spirit. This is how Jesus's mother, Mary, describes the process:

My soul magnifies the Lord and my spirit has rejoiced in God my Saviour… He who is mighty has done great things for me and holy is his name.[67]

In her life on earth Mary's soul magnified the Lord because her spirit rejoiced in all that God was doing in and for her. She was putting to death the things of the flesh and training her soul to follow the leading of her spirit as led by the Spirit of God.

Later in life, however, her soul at times took over when, for example, she joined with Jesus' half-brothers in seeking to *'take*

---

[65] John 4:24
[66] Romans 8: 13-14
[67] Like 1:47 and 49

Him away' because they considered Him *'beside himself'*. Thus, the NLT says: *'When his family heard what was happening, they tried to take him away. "He's out of his mind," they said.'* [68]

Hence the importance of being led by the Spirit onward through our earthly life. It is not for nothing the Lord says He will have no pleasure in one that turns back. And all this matters when we consider the afterlife.

For if our NDE teaches us anything, it is that heaven is where holiness is; that's why we were so thrilled to be there. Heaven is where God lives and He is holy. So, to live with Him we must be like Him. That means we too must be holy, and we can only be made holy through Jesus' death for us.

It also means that since God is Spirit it is only through our spirit when joined to his Spirit that we can enter and remain in his presence. And God has already joined the spirits of we who believe to his Spirit: *'But he who is joined to the Lord is one spirit with Him'.* [69]

Life then in the afterlife is through the spirit, not the soul. Contrary to what some teach, our soul does not accompany our spirit into the spirit world. It isn't needed. All things of God can be known through His Spirit co-joined with our spirit. And in the life to come, why would we want to know anything other than that which God could tell us? Could our own soul and mind tell us something better or greater than what God knows?

But, one minister argues, we need our soul in the afterlife because only through the soul we can exercise our five natural senses to explore the world beyond. However, the truth is that near-death experiencers can see, sense, feel and hear through their spirit.

---

[68] Mark 3:21
[69] 1 Corinthians 6:17

We don't need to take our soul on the trip; our spirit knows and can respond in every way necessary. In fact, the Spirit of God joined to our spirit is all-powerful. He created all things, sustains all things, knows all things, explores all things, is everywhere and empowers the spirits of those made perfect to know all He knows and do all that He does.

On return from our NDE excursion, we are more painfully aware of our many shortcomings. Of how much we need to change to qualify for residence in the heaven of the world beyond. And, from where most of us are, it seems very much a work still in progress.

This is where God's promise to the Old Testament temple re-builder, Zerubbabel, comes in. (As an aside, I wonder if Zerubbabel got his name because when his team started the rebuild, there was nothing but 'ze rubble').

You see, Zerubbabel laid the temple foundations then ran into big problems. The work became too difficult, a mountain seemingly impossible to climb. However, the Lord saw things differently. Remarkably, through the Prophet Zechariah, He tells Zerubbabel:

> *Not by might nor by power, but by my Spirit says the Lord of Hosts. Who are you, O, great mountain? Before Zerubbabel you shall become a plain. And he (Zerubbabel) shall bring forth the capstone (of the temple) with shouts of 'Grace, grace to it'.*[70]

---

[70] Zechariah 6-8

Chapter 19 - IS HEAVEN REALLY REAL?

But how do we know that the 'heaven' glimpsed in the near-death experience is real and not an illusion? Well for one thing, the majority of people who have an NDE, believe that it is heaven they experienced, however, briefly. Indeed, some go into lengthy descriptions of the abode above while others claim to have been taken on tours of it, escorted by no less a person than Jesus.

For another, Paul had his own out-of-body, near-death experience and says he went to heaven, the *'third heaven'* to be precise. He tells us about it in 2 Corinthians chapter 12:2-4 (NIV) saying:

> *I knew a man in Christ above 14 years ago was caught up to the third heaven. Whether it was in the body or **out of the body** I do not know – God knows. And I know this man – whether in the body or **apart from the body** I do not know, but God knows – was caught up to paradise. He heard inexpressible things that a man is not permitted to tell. I will boast of a man like that but I will not boast about myself except about my weaknesses.*

The Amplified Bible translation says *'this man'*, whom most believe is Paul, *'heard utterances beyond the power of man to put into words.'* And, for sure, many NDEers struggle to find words capable of explaining their profound and wonderful sensations on 'the other side'.

Now, was Paul's out-of-body trip also a near-death encounter? I believe it was, and not his only one at that. For, the apostle sent to '...*turn (the Gentiles) from darkness to light and from the power of Satan to God that they may receive forgiveness of sins...*' (Acts 26:18) was often violently attacked and suffered other great hardships.

In 2 Corinthians 11:23-25 he says he suffered five floggings by the Jews (40 stripes save one on each occurrence), three beatings with rods (it seems by Romans) and once was stoned at Lystra, where he had been used to miraculously heal a cripple who had been so from birth. Acts 14:19 (AMP) succinctly records what happened:

> *But some Jews arrived there from Antioch and Iconium (where Paul had earlier preached the gospel) and having persuaded the people and won them over, they stoned Paul and (afterward) dragged him out of the town, thinking that he was dead. But the disciples formed a circle around him and he got up and went back into town.*

Undoubtedly, this was a near-death experience, for Paul's attackers thought him dead. However, with the supernatural help of God through his disciples he *'got up'*, that is, he 'revived.' It was during this incident, I believe, that Paul, while unconscious and good as dead, made his out-of-body journey to Paradise as recorded in 2 Corinthians 12: 2-4.

Elsewhere in his writings, Paul speaks more about what he calls his *'deaths'* for which we could read 'near-deaths'. And the word *'deaths'* here translates the Greek word *thanatos*. To Paul then a 'near death' – a *thanatos* – is considered a real death but one from which he recovered. Fact is, he speaks more about his personal (near) deaths than other biblical authors. For example, in 2 Corinthians 11:23 he challenges those he calls *'false apostles'* saying:

> *Are they ministers of Christ? (I speak as a fool) I am more; in labours more abundant, in stripes (i.e., floggings) above measure, in prisons more frequent, **in deaths oft.***

The Amplified Bible renders the last three words as *'...**frequently at the point of death**'*.

Now if a man says he has been frequently at the point of death and *'in deaths oft'*, then he must stand out as the most frequent, near-death experiencer of all written history, if not of all time. If so, that would make Paul the best expert on what the near-death experience is and really means. His own journeys into and return from the world beyond also make him the go-to-authority on how to qualify for the after-life.

Now, there would be no NDEr who doesn't long with all his or her heart to return to the bliss and acceptance briefly experienced while out of the body. But, as said earlier, the grim truth is that each of us who returned to our earthly life were turned away from the Paradise we stumbled upon. And this is where Paul comes in. In his letters he spells out in detail just how sinners like you and I who have been turned back at the gates of heaven can at our final death enter them again, this time to stay.

In short, it means trusting Jesus as our Saviour and Lord. It means realising that both God and the Bible are true and that Jesus really was born of a virgin, that he lived a holy life wholly pleasing to God, that He died on the cross taking the punishment for our sins we should have suffered, that He rose from the grave, now rules over all from heaven and gives eternal life to those who believe and obey Him.

Importantly, Paul would have us follow his own example in trusting in the righteousness of Jesus which our Lord has graciously set to our account and can be received by us through faith. Which means, we must relinquish our own feeble attempts to make ourselves right and rely wholly on the Saviour's success instead.

Chapter 20 -
WHAT THE HELL?

If you don't believe in God, it follows that you also won't believe in heaven or hell. Yet vivid near-death experiences have convinced millions of previously ardent doubters that all three in fact truly exist. After all, how can they deny the existence of God once they have met Him? How can anyone deny the glory of heaven having tasted its peace, love and joy?

Come to that, how can we deny there is a hell when that word is constantly and vainly on all our lips? As an atheist, how can you deny the truth about hell if you have been taken on a demon-guided tour of the torment and fire of that place?

Author Bryan Melvin found he couldn't and, in his book, *'A Land Unknown: Hell's Dominion'* [71], tells a story every doubter in the dark side to the afterlife should read. Brought up in a loving Christian home, Bryan became an atheist and stayed one until he died from drinking cholera-poisoned water and found himself in hell. (You can buy his book or see interviews with him on the internet.)

Importantly, his experience shows that there really is a hell; that God doesn't send people there - they choose to go there themselves; that in hell, people really do suffer for the sins and evil they do in their life on earth; but that even in hell, those who

---

[71] Melvin, B.W., A Land Unknown: Hell's Dominion, 216 pages, published by Xulon Press, 2005, excerpts published online.

cry out to God can be saved. After all, didn't the Psalmist David say that even if he went to hell, he would find God there? [72]

Bryan's NDE began with a 'swoosh' when he floated above his body and realised he was dead. He no longer felt pain but entered a pleasant darkness. Floating towards a light, he found it was a Person clothed in white who then showed Bryan his life course, 'which revealed that I had no excuse'. I could only receive his sentence of judgement and I felt ashamed and wept. Then I noticed the deep gashes in his hands and feet'.

Bryan was told he was to see 'see another land for a time' and was taken down a tunnel which became a down-spiralling vortex. He fell to the ground, saw a house on a hill and was welcomed by 'people'. Was he in heaven? No, because it 'felt wrong'. Therefore, it must be hell. At this realisation the welcoming 'people' became translucent and beneath their guise it could be seen they were really foul creatures, demons. In terror Bryan voiced the words, 'Jesus Christ', over and over and 'I did not cease to do so until I left that place.'

A lizard-like demon then took Bryan on a journey through hell. He tore a hole in the horizon through which he led Bryan to downward-sloping land leading to 'an endless, circular spiral of misery'. On the sides of what Bryan now recognised as the 'pit'[73], often mentioned in Scripture, were tiers of 10-foot square cubes. Each housed an individual unable to escape his or her chamber.

Yet, Bryan found he could pass through the walls of his own cube. In their cells the entrapped people experienced restless boredom, anguish and hideous torments. Worse still, they were

---

[72] Psalm 139:7-12: Where shall I go from your Spirit? Or where shall I flee from your presence? If I ascend to heaven, you are there. If I make my bed in Sheol (hell) you are there (ESV).
[73] Ezekiel 32-17-32

deceived. Ghoulish entities created the illusion of people and places and things re-enacted from their former earthly lives.

Each trapped person resided alone, 'reaping in full measure whatever they had sown during their lives'. Unaware of each other – it seems nobody has friends in hell – they were alone. Each was learning they were banished from a loving God, the source of true life, and deserved such a fate because they had chosen to walk away from God when on earth. Thus, God in the afterlife could only give them what they had asked for: a place without God where they received the fruits of their doings in life.

Further down in the vortex, Bryan sees other examples of reaping what one has sown. A sailing ship captain who repeatedly lashed his crew in life, now in hell endures constant whippings from demons; others are trapped in fire, skin intact but repeatedly burning; a child-killer is constantly beaten, then swallowed by a snake and vomited out again to be beaten once more; a witch in former life, is held trapped alive in a coffin and scratching to get out.

Nazis are seen endlessly suffering the tortures and deaths they inflicted on others in their former lives and, most startling of all, Hitler is seen sitting in a fire in his cubicle. 'His flesh was burning and he had this hideous look on his face', Bryan says. 'It was like all the ovens of the concentration camps were now being used against him in a very hot fire. His flesh burned away but each time was renewed so it could be burned away again. And still, there was vicious, nasty anger in his eyes'.

The journey through hell draws to a close when the lizard demon tries to trap Bryan into a cubicle of his own. Bryan cries out repeatedly to God, and the 'Being in white' then lifts him up and away.

'One arm was under my shoulder and the other under my knees. Oh, the sensation of love, mercy, authority, power, justice and righteousness that overwhelmed me. I turned my head into the cleft of his shoulder and wept profusely'.

Bryan is carried back through the tunnel, to have his feet set on 'the rock' where he first met the 'Being in white', he now knows as Jesus, his Redeemer. He is then given a glimpse of heaven and told none can enter heaven except through the gate which is Jesus Himself. Suddenly, back in his body on earth, he cannot breathe until hit on the back, and then is rushed to hospital and takes months to recover.

So, what to make of all of that? Answer: If you persist in rejecting God in the now, hell for you is going to be all too real. In the afterlife, short of the mercy and forgiveness of God, which is available only through the shed blood of Jesus for your sin, and only when you turn to Him in repentance, you really will reap what you sow.

Chapter 21 -
HEALING FOR THE SPIRIT

Everybody has heard of post-traumatic stress disorder (PTSD) but few know what the Bible says about it. And despite the billions spent on supposed mental health cures, the sad truth is that few fully recover from the condition.

Why? Because the prescribed psychiatric procedures employed are based on treating PTSD as something that occurs only in the mind, the will and the emotions. But it doesn't. The real damage occurs in the human spirit, as a brief glance at scripture confirms. And only God can heal that.

But before we once again delve into the Bible, let's remember that no matter what terrible things we experience, even death, we can still pray unto God through our spirit. Even if we are out from a body which is lying unconscious on the operating table.

For, if Jonah prayed through his spirit to God from within the belly of a fish when dead, then so can you and I. That said, here's a sampling of what God's Word, the Bible, says about our spirit and how trauma affects it. A key verse is Proverbs 18:14:

> *The spirit of a man will sustain him in sickness but who can bear a **broken** spirit? (NKJV).*

> *The strong spirit of a man sustains him in bodily pain or trouble but a weak or **broken** spirit who can raise up or bear? (AMP).*

A wound to the spirit is grievous and deadly to the soul which of itself cannot compensate for the hurt. Thus Psalm 109:22 says:

> *For I am poor and needy and my heart is wounded within me (NKJV).*

> *Proverbs 15:13: A merry heart makes a cheerful countenance (face) but by sorrow of the heart the spirit is **broken** (NKJV).*

> *Proverbs 17:22: ... a cheerful mind works healing but a **broken** spirit dries up the bones (AMP).*

The underlying truth is that only God can cure the broken, crushed spirit. Billions of dollars are spent on man-devised treatments and therapies for the soul but mostly they only bandage unhealed wounds. We can say with Psalm 147:3: Only '... *He (God) heals the broken-hearted and binds up their wounds [curing their pains and sorrows]*' (AMP).

> *Psalm 34:18: The Lord is close to those who are of a broken heart and saves such as are crushed with sorrow for sin and are humbly and thoroughly penitent (AMP).*

When on earth, Jesus fulfilled the Prophet Isaiah's prediction that, as Messiah, He was sent to '... *bind up and heal the broken-hearted*' (Isaiah 61:1 and Luke 4:18, AMP). And if we will turn to Him with a whole heart repenting of our sin, He will still do so today. As said, the soul for most of us is how we view ourselves. It is the 'me' that I feel and know that is me. Now the soul has been rightly defined as comprising our mind, our will and our emotions. Or, that is, what we think, what we feel and determine to be and to do. But there is, or there can be, another 'me'. That is my spirit.

Proverbs 20:27 (NKJV) says: *'The spirit of a man is the lamp of the Lord searching all the inner depths of his heart'.* So, our spirit is described as a lamp, but it is one that can be put out. In the Book of Job the *'miserable comforter'* Bildad states of the wicked: *'The light is dark in his tent and his lamp beside him is put out'.* And Job himself in Job 21:17 says: *'How oft is the lamp of the wicked put out? How often does their destruction come upon them?'*

In Psalm 18:28 we read: *'For You will light my lamp. The Lord God will enlighten my darkness'.* 1 Corinthians 2:11 says: *'For what man knows the things of a man except the spirit of the man which is in him. Even so no-one knows the things of God except the Spirit of God'.* James 2:26: *'As the body without the spirit is dead so faith without works is dead'.*

So, we each have a spirit, but most of us live our life as though it does not exist. Short of a big wake-up call – and the near-death experience is just that – we live almost entirely in what we feel, what suits us, what we choose to believe and very little else. The 'other me', the spirit within, is rarely consulted. We do not search our heart to root out what is wrong with it. In fact, we are usually careful not to look into our heart at all.

As the Prophet Jeremiah wrote (Jeremiah 17:9): *'The heart is deceitful above all things and desperately wicked. Who can know it? I the Lord search the heart, I test the mind, even to give every man according to his ways, according to the fruit of his doings.'*

Ephesians 2:5 insists that short of God of relighting our lamp - our spirit – by *'quickening'* us afresh, we remain *'dead in trespasses and sins'.* Only those whose spirit has been brought back to life by God can say that they have been saved by grace and *'made alive together with Christ'* - in the spirit, that is. Fact is, God put a spirit, part of his Spirit, and a holy spirit at that, within us when we were yet in the womb. Without it we would not have lived at all because without the spirit the body is dead. Thus, God is the *father of all spirits* (Hebrews 12:9). Scientist and author Henry M. Morris, Ph. D, says:

Human parents transmit physical characteristics to their offspring, but our spiritual attributes come from God, for He is 'the Father of spirits'. Paul recognized that all men are *the offspring of God* (Acts 17:29), and that each man is still *the image and glory of God* (1 Corinthians 11:7). Thus, our spirit/soul nature, as distinct from our body of physical/mental flesh, has come from God, who created it and united it with our body, evidently at the moment of physical conception in the womb. It is obvious that the *image of God*, man's spirit/soul nature, could not be transmitted genetically via the 'genetic code' and the DNA molecules, for these are simply complex chemicals programmed to transmit only the physical and mental attributes of the ancestors to the children. Nevertheless, the spirit/soul attributes of each person also seem to be associated inseparably with the body from conception onwards, continuing so until separated again at death, when the spirit goes *to be absent from the body, and to be present with the Lord* (2 Corinthians 5:8), leaving the body behind. In the meantime, however, the *image of God* in man is marred by its incorporation in our *sinful flesh* for *the body is dead because of sin* (Romans 8:3, 10). By this union of flesh and spirit, man inherits Adam's fallen nature as well as his mortal body, and both are in need of salvation. Christ *'gave himself for us, that he might redeem us from all iniquity.'* (Titus 2:14)

Therefore, we, like Paul, can pray that our *'whole spirit and soul and body be preserved blameless unto the coming of our Lord Jesus Christ'* (1 Thessalonians 5:23). But we must ask, how did our spirit 'die'? Answer: we ourselves put it to death by refusing to heed the Spirit's voice within and insisting on having our own way.

As you may have noticed, even babies want to have their own way. By the time the infant has grown to be a toddler, nobody needs to tell him to say 'No' to Mum or Dad - that comes naturally, or unnaturally, depending on your viewpoint. Nor does he need anyone to teach him to lie, steal or rebel. Again, these all come naturally from the fallen nature we have all inherited from sinning Adam. And as we grow up, the more we sin, the less we hear the still, small voice within telling us of a better way to go. By adulthood, our spirit has become a switched off radio and we make ourselves deaf to the inner broadcast voice of God.

At this point, it is only God who, by breaking into our hearts and thus intervening in our lives, can switch it back on again. And this He does for all who ask Him.

Chapter 22 -
IS REINCARNATION THE ANSWER?

Stand by for a shock if you are a Christian and perhaps even if you are not. For it seems the Bible does teach reincarnation. Or does it? Certainly, it records that the spirit of a deceased man can live again in another person. But, if scripture exemplifies reincarnation, it does so in a way that is not popularly understood. So, this chapter asks whether it is reincarnation that follows death as many believe, or is resurrection the only real hope of living again in a body upon the earth?

It is an important issue because it seems many return from their near-death experience convinced that after death, they will be reincarnated as a matter of course to live again as a new and different person. What's more, many also believe their present life is only a temporary episode in a cycle of reincarnations in which they have lived earlier lives and will live again in future ones. For Buddhists and Hindus such reincarnation is the essence of their belief.

The sober fact is that 33 per cent of Americans believe in reincarnation. Numbers of people in New Age and other esoteric circles also believe and tell, sometimes in surprising detail, of the existence they say they had in previous lives.

Millions of Hindus hold that those who do evil in their present life will be punished by being reincarnated in a lesser form, as a poor person, an animal, a snake or even an insect.

Buddhists who, like Hindus, base their view on the doctrine of *karma,* hold that the soul seeking enlightenment may well undergo several different lives before ultimately achieving 'Nirvana', the blissful state of self-extinction said to occur as one is absorbed into the spirit of the universe.

Karma, simply put, is the conviction that men and women suffer illness and evil because of the wrongs they have done. Popularly, it's known as 'what goes around comes around'. But for me, the Bible puts it better, saying: *'Be not deceived. God is not mocked; for whatever a man sows that he will also reap. For he who sows to his flesh (i.e., his bodily, soulish nature) will of the flesh reap corruption but he who sows to the Spirit will of the Spirit reap everlasting life'.* [74]

So, is reincarnation the answer to the sinful human condition? To answer that, let's ask another question. Even if we can be reincarnated into a series of future lives how many such lives would it take for us to get our behaviour absolutely holy and right? Especially if we have already begun this quest in earlier lives and still fall seriously short of the mark in our present life?

And surely, if reincarnation is true, in the thousands of years mankind has existed, some among us must have reached absolute perfection. Shouldn't such people be showing up as a growing proportion of noticeably more righteous people in each new generation? Find some if you can. Come to that, are there any alive at all who are perfect today?

Take a sharp look at yourself, those close to you and then peruse the news headlines and latest crime statistics to find the answer. It is that you, I and they are all still *'under sin'* [75] and in

---

74 Galatians 6:7-8
75 Romans 3:9.

a need of a Saviour? And, as I was told, long ago, there is only one Saviour available. His name is Jesus Christ. You see:

> *There is none righteous, no not one. There is none who understands. There is none who seek after God. They have all turned aside. They have together become unprofitable. There is none who does good, no, not one'* [76]

While many believe mankind is slowly 'getting better', the evidence is that no such 'evolution' – a word much used by its adherents to explain the supposed process of reincarnation – is taking place. We are not improving. Far from it. As unsaved people we are still as wicked, violent and hateful at heart as we were thousands of years ago. Furthermore, believing in reincarnation by itself does little to improve our moral state. Short of the heart-changing power of the Spirit of Jesus Christ, our Saviour, we struggle in vain to overcome our evil inner nature and its sin.

So, what does the Bible say about reincarnation? Can a person be born again into a new life? This may come as a shock but, yes, it seems they can. However, such rebirth takes place in this life, not the next and if the biblical evidence is examined it shows that reincarnation – if that is the right word – happens only to a very small number of special and unique individuals. So what hope is there of a blessed afterlife for the more mundane rest of us?

Answer: two things. Firstly, entry into the kingdom of God or the kingdom of heaven (come down to earth) that Jesus and Paul spoke of. And, secondly, through the biblical promise of resurrection, both spiritual and physical. As Jesus said:

---

[76] Romans 3: 10-12.

> *Except a man be born again he cannot see the kingdom
> of God…Except a man be born of water and of the
> Spirit he cannot enter the kingdom of God. That which
> is born of the flesh (our sinful nature) is flesh, and that
> which is born of the Spirit it is spirit.*[77]

Questions must be asked if reincarnation is held to be a common after-death experience for most people. For example, what about the verse where we are told that the name of Jesus is the only name given under heaven, whereby we must be saved. Do those who refuse his offer of salvation - and so do not know Him as their Saviour and Lord - get a second chance of life after death? And, how about the Bible verse that says he who does not believe in Jesus as Saviour is *'condemned already because he has not believed on the name of the only begotten Son of God'?*[78]

What of the verse that warns that those who reject God, won't repent and seek his forgiveness, or refuse to accept his salvation become *'…brute beasts made to be taken and destroyed … (they) shall utterly perish in their own destruction'*[79]? Question: If you are condemned and destroyed can you be reincarnated?

That much said, it must be admitted that the Bible does give examples of what might be seen as reincarnation in some very few individuals who, it seems, are special cases. For example, Jesus identified John the Baptist as *'Elijah who was to come'.*[80] The passage reads:

> *For all the prophets and the law prophesied. And if you
> are willing to receive it, he is Elijah who was to come.*

---

[77] John 3:3--6
[78] John 3:15-17
[79] 2 Thessalonians 2:12
[80] Matthew 11:13-14

Now, several centuries separate the life of Elijah and that of John the Baptist. Yet John was only conceived after an angel appeared to tell an aged childless couple, Zacharias and Elisabeth (his barren wife), they would have a son who would…

> *… be great in the sight of the Lord … be filled with the Holy Spirit from his mother's womb… turn many of the children of Israel to the Lord their God … (and) go before Him in the spirit and power of Elijah to turn the hearts of the fathers to the children.* [81]

And the Bible has it that it is also Elijah who, along with Moses, appeared on the Mount of Transfiguration when Jesus was transformed before three chosen disciples to appear as He will be as the future coming King of Glory.[82]

Note that John the Baptist, who had the spirit of Elijah, had been dead for more than a year by the time of this occurrence, having been executed by Herod the king. So, although John the Baptist had lived and moved in the power and spirit of Elijah one concludes it was not he, but Elijah himself who appeared on the mount. And, if that's the case, was it reincarnation or a spiritual manifestation? Reader, you be the judge.

What's more, according to Jesus, Elijah is to return again in the future '…*before the coming of the great and dreadful day of the Lord*'[83] (when God's wrath is poured out on an unrepentant mankind). This He explained when his disciples asked Him, saying…

> *…Why then do the scribes say that Elijah must come first? Jesus answered and said to them, 'Indeed Elijah*

---

[81] Luke 1:15-17
[82] Matthew 17:1-9
[83] Malachi 4:5

is coming first and will restore all things. But I say unto you that Elijah has come already; and they did not know him but did to him whatever they wished. Likewise, the Son of Man is also about to suffer at their hands'. Then the disciples understood that He spoke to them of John the Baptist. [84]

So, when he comes again Elijah, in one form or another, will have had three appearances on earth. But none of them can be said to constitute a reincarnation. Why? Because Elijah has never died. You see, when his ministry on earth as a prophet came to a close, a chariot of fire appeared separating him from his successor Elisha, and Elijah was drawn up into heaven by a whirlwind.[85] Thus, he is one of only two men mentioned in the Bible as having been taken up into heaven by God without dying. The other is Enoch whose amazing story is told below:

So, all the days of Enoch were three hundred and sixty-five years. And Enoch walked with God; and he was not, for God took him. [86]

Furthermore, scripture also draws a veil over the beginnings of Elijah. We are not told who his parents were; rather the Bible says he was a *'Tishbite, of the inhabitants of Gilead. '[87]* According to the LXX, he was a *'stranger'* in Tishbi of Gilead. Fact is, the Bible neither mentions Elijah's birth nor his death. Rather, as said, it states that the Prophet Elijah left the earth when a chariot of fire appeared and he was taken up into heaven by a whirlwind.

However, there is record of both the birth and death of Moses who, much later, as we have seen, appeared with Elijah

---

84 Matthew 17:10-12
85 2 Kings 2:11
86 Genesis 5:23-24
87 1 Kings 17:1

and Jesus on the Mount of Transfiguration. Of his earthly demise Deuteronomy 34:5 simply says:

So Moses the servant of God died there in the land of Moab, according to the word of the Lord. And He buried him in a valley in the land of Moab opposite Beth-Peor but no one knows his grave to this day.

Arguably, then, Moses' reappearance at Jesus' transfiguration could be seen as a reincarnation, but again there is another possible explanation. You see, the return to earth of Jesus as the Son of Man, was still future in the Lord's time on earth. Indeed, it is still future today. So, it was a vision of the future that the disciples saw, on the Mount of Transfiguration, not an actual physical occurrence at that time. Being thus fast forwarded into future prophesied events is not a unique biblical phenomenon. It happened to Isaiah, Daniel, and the Apostle John among others.

For the record, the word reincarnation is found nowhere in the Bible, but the word resurrection appears 40 times in the King James Version. What's more, in scripture believers are promised both a spiritual resurrection in this life and a resurrection of their whole body in the life to come.

Certainly, it was a spiritual resurrection, if not a full near-death experience that occurred to the famous 18th-century English preacher Charles Wesley. His story is told in the next chapter.

Chapter 23 - DID CHARLES WESLEY HAVE AN NDE?

In one of his hymns, famed evangelist and prolific song composer Charles Wesley, records his own awakening to the 'light', apparently after experiencing near death from a severe illness. He writes:

Long my imprisoned spirit lay
Fast bound in sin and nature's night;
Thine eye diffused a quick'ning ray,
I woke, the dungeon flamed with light;
My chains fell off, my heart was free;
I rose, went forth and followed Thee.
No condemnation now I dread;
Jesus, and all in Him is mine!
Alive in Him, my living Head
And clothed in righteousness divine
Bold I approach th'eternal throne
And claim the crown, through Christ my own.

Charles Wesley wrote nearly 9,000 hymns. What's more, in the mid-1700s, Charles, with his brother John and fellow evangelist George Whitefield, was used of God to bring millions to Christ on both sides of the Atlantic. With amazing energy and at huge personal cost, the trio preached into being, a return to belief in God and his salvation by grace through faith alone in the shed blood of the Saviour, the Lord Jesus Christ, that wrought huge social change for the better in both Britain and America.

The Industrial Revolution that mechanised manufacture and, despite its sins and failures, ultimately improved living standards around the globe, was sparked by the Wesley-Whitefield revivals. You see, the value of human life took on new meaning in the understanding that …

> *…God, who is rich in mercy, for his great love with which He loved us, even when we were dead in trespasses has made us alive together with Christ (by grace ye are saved).*[88]

Every soul was now precious. The 'awakening' to new life was not just for a chosen churchy few but for everyone. And God was concerned to bless the poor and downtrodden in this life as much as He promised them bliss in the next. The Wesleys insisted that, as the Apostle John said, '*…Jesus Christ the Righteous … is the atoning sacrifice for our sins, and not only for ours, but also for the sins of the whole world*' (NIV). [89]

In the wake of this remarkable revival came wonderful, life-improving inventions, ranging through James Watt's steam engine, Arkwright's powered spinning frame, Hargreaves' spinning Jenny to Davies' miner's lamp, Stephenson's locomotive and many more. The Industrial Revolution raised millions out of serfdom and extended the average life span from 36 to 45. Its benefits were felt around the globe.

---

[88] Ephesians 2:5
[89] 1 John 2:1-2

Following it, also came many social reforms, unequalled before or since for number. Voting rights were extended, first to all property owners, then to all men and, later to women too. Trade unions were legalised and allowed to picket; slave and child labour were abolished and inhuman working conditions eased. Education and health care came to be provided for all. Local councils were empowered to provide the structural necessities of life. Importantly, it was believed by Christians that all these changes for the better were the munificent gifts of the Lord Jesus Christ, heeding the fervent prayers of those who had newly put their trust in Him.

Yet it all began with the personal 'awakenings' of Charles and John Wesley within days of each other back in 1738. And, be it noted, Charles' own conversion experience has the hallmarks of a near-death if not out-of-body experience. Whether he had a full-on near-death encounter is unclear but actually, he had been seriously ill for weeks and the disease reached a crisis point at the time of his 'awakening'. In the above hymn he writes of his 'imprisoned spirit' being 'fast bound in sin and nature's night' and likens his condition to being in a 'dungeon'.

Could it be that Wesley, like so many NDEers, experienced the dark tunnel of life re-examination before seeing the 'quickening ray diffused by the eye of God' that made his dungeon 'flame with light'? Certainly, his encounter with God not only changed his heart but, ultimately, that of the world around him. For, after 'seeing the light', his preaching no longer urged doing good works to earn a place in heaven. Instead, he invoked the need to be 'born again' or 'born from above' to qualify for eternal life, just as Jesus told Nicodemus he needed to be.[90]

So, is that the real message from the light seen at the end of the tunnel in the near-death experience? I believe it is. We must be 'born again'- that is changed in heart - if we are to see, enter, and above all, remain in the glorious light of the afterlife that is essentially, and only, with and through God. And when we are born again, we not only have peace with God but also, like Wesley, perhaps the God-given power to change both ourselves and the world around us.

Now, there's one thing Charles Wesley was very clear about that most NDEers are not. It was his 'spirit', not his soul, which awoke when the light flamed. Actually, he treats his soul and his body together as the 'dungeon' that until then had kept his spirit 'fast bound in sin and nature's night'. Nowhere in the hymn, *'And can it be that I should gain an interest in the Saviour's blood?'* does he even mention the soul. Rather, he declares that once the light broke into his life, '…My chains fell off, my heart was free. I rose went forth and followed Thee'.

Consequently, he now no longer dreads condemnation but, 'alive in Christ, his living Head' he is clothed 'in righteousness divine', approaches the 'eternal throne' and claims the crown (of living in God's bliss for eternity, I suggest) 'through Christ my own'. And it is clear he knew that while it is the soul (our mind will and emotions) that is saved in this life, it is in our spirit that we have consciousness in the world after death.

So, what of the soul in the afterlife? Is it truly dead or just asleep? The next chapter addresses this important question.

---

[90] John 3:7

Chapter 24 -
DOES OUR SOUL SLEEP?

Do you believe in soul sleep? Seventh Day Adventists and some other Christians do. They hold that upon death the believer's soul, spirit and body sleep in the grave until resurrection. An official SDA explanation says:

> Seventh-day Adventists believe that the word "soul" does not refer to a part of a person that is immortal, but to the person itself. In Genesis, when God breathed into Adam the breath of life, several versions say he "became a living soul." … Basically, instead of a person going to heaven or hell at death, or becoming a ghost or an angel, they believe that the person ceases to exist. But because God created each person in the first place and knows who each of us is, he can resurrect or recreate us at the Second Coming without a problem, so it is as if we were asleep all the time we were dead, and that is why it is compared to sleep: the next thing we know after dying, Jesus is calling us from our graves. Adventists point out that Jesus himself compared death to a sleep when he went to Jairus' house and raised his daughter back to life. He told the mourners that she was only sleeping.

On the other hand, most folk believe the soul is immortal; that it is in the soul that our consciousness lives on after death. For example, Michael Newton Ph. D. in his recently published book, *'The Journey of Souls'*, asserts that our souls live on for ever, an afterlife continuance punctuated only by physical deaths and subsequent incarnation into new lives.

Dr. Newton's book blurb hails his ground-breaking 'discoveries' '...that reveal for the first time the mystery of life in the spirit world after death on earth – proof that our consciousness survives'.

These 'amazing insights into what happens to us between lives' stem, he says, from using 'a special hypnosis technique to reach the hidden memories' of some 29 subjects whose stories are told in the book. Topics covered include: how it feels to die, what it feels like after death, the truth about 'spiritual guides', the fate of 'disturbed souls', the different levels of souls in the afterlife – supposedly there's a hierarchy - and how to choose another body to return to earth.

But what if all that is an illusion? What if the 'spiritual guides' are actually demons? – for the Bible warns such evil spirit beings are real – implanting visions and memories of previous lives that actually never occurred?

Scripture teaches – and we know it's true from bitter experience - that there are powerful '...*rulers of the darkness of this age ... spiritual hosts of wickedness in the heavenly places'.* [91] So, there are master spirits who rule over our darkened world. These operate as minions of Satan who, Jesus said, was the evil '*prince of this world'*[92]. Paul calls him '...*the god of this world'*[93] and '...*the prince of the power of the air'.*[94] The Apostle John warns, *'The whole world lies in the power of the evil one'.*[95]

---

[91] Ephesians 6:12

[92] John 14:30

[93] 2 Corinthians 4:4

[94] Ephesians 2:2

[95] 1 John 5:19

And if they can hoodwink and bring destruction on us on earth, why should we not believe they are capable of doing the same in the lower spiritual realms of the afterlife? Especially when the Apostle Paul says that the spirit world is their home and operations centre. Thus, in Ephesians 6:12, he writes:

> *For we wrestle not against flesh and blood but against principalities, against powers, against the rulers of the darkness of this world, against spiritual wickedness in* ***high places.***

It's this struggle, the battle between good (God) and evil (the devil and his fellow wicked spirits), that makes it hard to sort the wheat from the chaff, the truth from the lies, when evaluating near-death experiences.

You see, Satan still operates today as *'...the prince of the power of the air, the spirit who now works in the sons of disobedience'.*[96] He steers the world's course and tries to lead each person to trust in themselves and in him rather in God. His bag of tricks includes the lie that the soul lives on after death, that man is basically good, and that evolution is the key to him becoming a higher being. But Paul writes that we all have walked *'...in trespasses and sins according to the course of this world'* and have thus become *'...dead in trespasses and sins.'*[97]

Simply put, that means we have killed the holy spirit God put within us at conception (Note that scripture says that God *'is the father of all spirits'*[98] and since God has only one spirit, the Holy Spirit, it is a portion of that spirit of His that we are given). Sadly, by sinning, we soon shut that spirit down. From

---

[96] Ephesians 2:2
[97] Ephesians 2:1
[98] Hebrews 12:9

then on, like a switched off two-way radio, our spirit does not talk to God, nor hear from Him.

And that is evidenced by our not wanting to know God or have anything to do with Him. Romans 3:11 says, *'There is none who understands, none who seek after God'*. And the reason they don't is that their spirit is dead because of sin.

Fact is, only God can bring our spirit back to life and this only by breathing His own Spirit into it. He does so by *'quickening'* our spirit or making it alive once more.

> *And you [He made alive], when you were dead [slain] by [your] trespasses and sins. (AMP)*

> *And you hath He quickened who were dead in trespasses and sins. (KJV)* [99]

Although the soul is saved in this quickening process, such salvation occurs only if first our spirit is resurrected from within.

So, does our soul sleep, not die, after death? Fact is, nowhere does the Bible say the soul sleeps after death. Always it is the person as a whole who sleeps after death. For example, when Lazarus fell ill and died, Jesus said: *'Our friend Lazarus sleeps but I go that I may wake him up.'* [100] In 1 Thessalonians 4:13-14, Paul speaks of those who have *'fallen asleep'* and who *'sleep in Jesus'* but he doesn't mention their souls.

And, when it comes to consciousness after death in the Bible it is always the **spirit,** not the soul, that lives on. Two examples are:

Luke 23:46: Jesus dying on the cross said, *'...Father into your hands I commit my* **spirit** *'*.

---

[99] Ephesians 2:1
[100] John 11:11

Acts 7:55: Stephen being stoned to death cried out: *'Lord Jesus, receive my* **spirit***'.*

So, it is a forgotten truth, even among many Christians, that it is only in the spirit that believers can go to be with Christ after death. It is a mistake to think one's soul also makes the journey. It doesn't.

But the soul will live again when the believer is resurrected as a whole being – *spirit, soul and body* [101] - in time to come.

---

[101] 1 Thessalonians 5:23

Chapter 25 -
HAVE VISION, WILL TRAVEL

Do people always have to die, or nearly die, to experience the spirit world? Surprisingly, the answer is no, they don't. But they do have to be careful that it is through Christ and not some other spirit that they traverse the spiritual realm. And, while the soul (our mind, will and emotions) can produce and experience all sorts of phenomena, it is only through our spirit, not our soul, that we safely encounter reality in the world beyond.

Actually, God wants everyone to live in his spirit even while alive in the body on earth. He also wants us all to experience all of the spiritual blessings He has made available to all who, in Christ, have been lifted up into *'heavenly places'*, the Bible word for the spirit world. Thus, we are told:

> *Blessed be the God and Father of our Lord Jesus Christ who has blessed us with every spiritual blessing in the heavenly places in Christ just as He chose in Him before the foundation of the world that we should be holy and without blame before Him in love.* [102]

Being spiritually blessed in *'heavenly places'* is a true out-of-the-body experience while still alive in our body on earth. And there are yet more OBEs mentioned in Scripture. The Bible records many instances of called-of-God men going into a

---

[102] Ephesians 1:3-4

trance, seeing visions; even being transported in the spirit from one place to another. Examples shortly.

Meanwhile, let's realise afresh that the only reason NDEers are able to leave their bodies, travel up the dark tunnel and reach the realm of light is because they do it in their spirit. What's more, some near-death experiencers have travelled widely around the earth and even into space during their world-beyond excursions.

For example, in his book, *'Return from Tomorrow'*, Dr. George Ritchie tells that he was training to be an army doctor when he became ill and died from pneumonia. Nine minutes later he revived to tell of his amazing NDE while 'dead'.

He leaves his body, not realising it is his, and, wanting to go to Richmond, Virginia, to start college, finds himself flying in the air. He effortlessly reaches a city to find he has lost his bodily 'solidness'. Concerned, he flies back to the hospital to see his lifeless body in the morgue and realises he is dead.

Jesus suddenly appears, emanating light and love and conducts a life review in which, not Jesus, but George, is found to be judging himself. Doesn't the Bible say that if we judge ourselves then we will not be judged?[103] Jesus then gives George a flying tour of four different aspects of the afterlife. He sees the spirit of a woman who died from nicotine poisoning desperately seeking to get a cigarette from factory workers but cannot.

Elsewhere he sees the spirit of a boy vainly beg forgiveness from a living girl but she is completely unaware of his presence. Thence to a bar full of hard drinking sailors where spirits try in vain to get a drink for themselves. When a drunken sailor passes out, immediately an alcoholic spirit jumps into him.

---

[103] Romans 11:31

Jesus then takes George to a place where the spirits of people are in deep hypnotic sleep. This because they believe they must sleep after death until Jesus returns. Elsewhere George is shown angry spirits vainly trying to fight and hurt each other. Many verbally abuse others. In arguments over religious or political points, spirits even try to kill each other. George now realises that all this is hell, where spirits still have earthly desires that cannot be met in the reality of the very spiritual afterlife.

On to a vast university and library where spirits engage in art or research. George is told these persons are those who have grown beyond selfish desires while on earth. 'Is this heaven?' he asks. No, he is told, it's not, because these scholarly spirits can no more see Jesus than those elsewhere in hell can, for the simple reason they did not put their trust in Him in their earthly lives. Consequently, they cannot or will not bring themselves to do so now in the afterlife. It seems seeing and knowing Jesus, or not knowing Him, can determine one's afterlife destiny.

Flying now into outer space toward a brilliantly lit city, George senses this is the *'heavenly Jerusalem'* of the biblical Book of Revelation and learns this is where people go who have become Christ-like on earth. In this heaven, the focus is on love, but he is not allowed to enter it. Jesus then shows George the future of the earth, and he is returned to his body.

We must ask, is such speedy travel on earth and flying about in heaven for real or a figment of the imagination? If it's for real, and in our spirit, we can explore a vast universe at the speed of light or even faster, then we would expect to read about this being experienced by people in the Bible. And, amazingly, we do.

While alive on earth the Prophet Ezekiel was lifted up by the Spirit to see the *'glory of the Lord from his place'*. [104] He saw, or heard, the wheels of the Lord's chariot, the living creatures that accompanied it and then was taken by the Spirit from heaven down to the Israelite captives by the River Chebar. Along with Daniel and several other biblical characters he saw the Lord in glory, just as the Apostle John did, and *'fell at his feet as though dead'*.[105] In other words, John also had an OBE, for, as he says, he was taken up in the Spirit on the Lord's Day, meaning that he was transported forward in time to be shown what will happen in the future *'day of the Lord'*.[106]

The deacon Philip also has a story of spiritual transportation to tell. Having baptised the newly saved eunuch, he was whisked away by the Spirit of the Lord from the Jerusalem to Gaza Road and was then found at Azotus many miles away.

What do we learn from all this? Answer: that in the afterlife our spirit can, as led by the Lord and in his Spirit, fly vast distances in an instant and visit many different states of being while being weightless and unrestricted. Further evidence is that Jesus Himself, after his resurrection, and thus in a real but resurrected spiritual body, passed through solid walls and locked doors to suddenly appear before the disciples.[107]

Importantly, it is in our spirit that we can be made perfect and presented faultless before God in heaven. But that's not to say we can't be resurrected later on as both soul and spirit in a

---

[104] Ezekiel 2:12-15
[105] Revelation 1:17
[106] Revelation 1:10. When the Hebrew phrase 'day of the Lord' is rendered in Greek it becomes 'the Lord's day', not a reference to worshipping God on Sunday but describing the day of judgement on earth to come.
[107] John 20: 19 and 26

body like Jesus's and perhaps even then, at the speed of light, go where we will.

Meantime, Paul wrote that when *'that which is perfect is come'* we will *'see face to face'*, and not know in part but *'know just as I also am known'*.[108] Now to know as God knows us, and to also know everything He knows, requires a huge expansion of our knowledge. And this is just what people experiencing near death also briefly find.

Almost instantaneously, their consciousness is vastly expanded to take in amazing vistas of truth that, as the Apostle Paul intimated, it is not *'lawful'* for a man to utter. By which I believe he meant that it was all but impossible to explain in this life what God shows us in the next. Why? Because it's so profoundly greater than anything we can think or imagine in our earth-bound existence here below:

> *Eye hath not seen, nor ear heard, nor have entered into the heart of man the things which God has prepared for those who love Him... Now we have received not the spirit of the world, but the Spirit who is from God that we might know the things that are freely given to us of God.* [109]

> *He [God] that spared not his own Son, but delivered Him up for us all, how shall He not with Him also give us freely all things.*[110]

In the life to come receiving all that God has to give, which is all that He has and is, will be hugely enjoyable:

---

108 1 Corinthians 13:9-12
109 1 Corinthians 2:10-12
110 Romans 8:32

> *You will show me the path of life; in your presence is fullness of joy; at your right hand are pleasures for evermore.*[111]

Just what is this pleasure, this ecstasy that God will give us in the life to come and that is also experienced all too briefly by NDErs on their cut-short visit to Paradise? First of all, I believe it is being able to come face to face and up close to Jesus Himself, the source of all love, forgiveness and everything that is good. Second, it will be the sheer bliss of being able to accomplish with miraculous ease the good things we have tried to bring about in our earth life but too often struggled in vain to achieve. You see, among the above-mentioned *'all things'* given to us by God will be his power. Miracles will be at our beck and call. In the afterlife, saints made holy by the blood of Jesus will, as He said, be able to:

> *...say unto this mountain "move from here to there" and it will move, and nothing will be impossible for you.*[112]

The word *'will'* here, makes clear use of such miraculous power is largely future. The one condition to be met is having *'faith as the grain of a mustard seed'*[113]. In our present life such faith is hard come by. Some miracles occur, but often Christians find fulfilment of much they longed for, hoped for and prayed for is postponed. Their faith is tested, their hope perfected by delay. The Bible calls it the *'trial of your faith'* and clearly states that God's Old Testament heroes *'...having obtained a good*

---

[111] Psalm 16:11
[112] Matthew 17:20-20; 21:21
[113] Matthew 13:31

testimony through faith did not receive [in this life] the promise... that ... they should be made perfect'.[114]

But in the life to come, briefly sensed in the near-death experience, both believers and their faith are found perfect. Thus, Hebrews 12:23 speaks of coming to *'the spirits of just men made perfect'* and Hebrews 2:5 tells us that God has *'...not put the world to come of which we speak in subjection to angels'* but to men who have been redeemed from sin by the blood of Jesus and made holy in order to rule.[115]

So, Jesus not only *'tasted death for everyone'* to ensure there can be a life hereafter, He also did so *'to bring many sons to glory',* the glory that will see mankind *'crowned with glory and honour'* and *'set over the works of your [God's] hands; You have put all things in subjection under his feet'*[116]

And that, if you will accept it, is our true destiny in life after death. It is to be at God's right hand, found in the Person of Jesus Christ, and ruling and reigning with Him over the entire universe. Best of all we will be always in His presence. But you don't have to wait until going to heaven to experience the joy to be found in the presence of Jesus. That can be found while still in your body on earth.

Jesus has promised *'... where two or three are gathered together in my name, I am there in the midst of them'.* [117] And week by week, as they worship God together, believers, who know Jesus as Saviour and Lord and are filled and led by his Spirit, enter into and palpably experience his presence.

The good news is that the joy of that will be unceasing in the life to come.

---

[114] Hebrews 11:39-40
[115] Hebrews 2:7-8
[116] Hebrews 2:7-8
[117] Matthew 18:20

Chapter 26 - BUT IT'S SO EASY TO REPENT

It seems that whether in this life or the next, God has made it easy for everybody to come to Him. That's why we near-death experiencers are powerfully drawn towards the love, grace, acceptance and forgiveness flowing from the 'Beings in white' we encounter in the spirit world.

Yes, it's easy to want to come close to God the Father and Jesus in the afterlife. Especially when you've just been shown how your sins and failures in the life here below can be forgiven and put right. Most everybody on the journey into the 'world to come' wants to draw close to the Holy Ones they sense are there and long to stay with them forever. And, as we have seen, hardened atheists who on earth refused to believe in God or the afterlife, repent when they actually meet Him in their NDE.

Now to repent means to change one's beliefs. It means to bow to the greater reality one has refused to admit until irrefutably confronted with it. Actually, no-one has to wait until a near-death experience or actual death in order to do so. One can get right with God in this life right now. Indeed, He longs for us to do so.

And down the centuries, since Jesus died on the cross for all our sins and rose again to give those who believe in Him eternal life, countless millions have put their trust in Him, had their sins forgiven and begun a new life of being changed to be like Him by the power of his Spirit living within them.

So, why is it so hard for most of us alive on earth to likewise repent – change our wrong ideas – and be saved? Answer in a nutshell: Because we are too proud and worried about what others might think to do so. For to ask Jesus to save us from the mess of sin, hate and failure most of us have already made of our lives, is a humbling experience. It requires admitting we got it wrong about who God is, about who we are and why He created us in the first place. It means asking Him to forgive us.

I, for one, had to be dragged kicking and screaming to do so. But let me say, to be accepted and forgiven by God and have his Spirit of peace come to live inside you, is one of the greatest experiences that can ever happen to you in this life or the next. And that, surely, is the reason many of us have had a near-death experience.

We have found, as I did, that life without peace with God through Jesus Christ is hard. Short of repenting and putting our faith in Him we remain uneasy, troubled by guilt, fearing the future and feeling that we are not the persons we should be. Worst of all, there is a deep emptiness inside that cannot be filled with all the present world has to offer. We know instinctively that we were destined to accomplish greater, higher things; in short, to serve God. But we find it hard to take the simple course of admitting we were wrong.

But let me say, it can be easy. Just a simple prayer, like the one I, after a long struggle, learned to pray, will get you started. It went like this:

> 'Oh God, I've made a mess of my life and now I'm in trouble. Please forgive me for rejecting you all these years, for despising the riches of your grace and for-

giveness. I confess my sin of not believing in You and ask You to forgive me and come into my life and take control of me as my Saviour and Lord. Thank You for dying for my sin so that I don't have to. It's in your name Jesus, that I ask. Amen.'

If you mean it when you pray such a prayer, peace from God will enter your heart, your fear of death and being judged and condemned will depart, and you will know the joy of being welcomed home by a loving Father. Why not give it a go?

Chapter 27 - SOME OTHER WAY?

Is it possible to get to heaven and stay on in bliss without Jesus? Aside from Him, is there some other way to both enter and stay in the Paradise of the afterlife? Recognised researchers into, and authorities on, the near-death experience seem to think there is. To them it matters not whether the 'Being in light' most NDErs encounter is recognised as Buddha, Mohammed, a Hindu saint or deity or in some cases, Jesus.

The upshot, they say, is the same. For they hold there really is an afterlife and the news about it is all good. Heaven in their view is thus open to all regardless of who or what they believe. Consequently, they say, there is no need to fear death; or judgement in its aftermath. It's just the gateway to a splendid afterlife in which all our dreams can come true. For them the best is yet to come when we die regardless of whether we know Jesus as Saviour and Lord or not.

But is that really so? If it is, then both the Bible and Jesus have got it wrong and the Lord who died for our sins is guilty of having terribly misled humanity about heaven and what really happens to us after death. However, if He is right, then it is most of us who have got it wrong, terribly wrong, and unless we heed what He says, we may find ourselves shut out from the afterlife Paradise we all really want as our eternal home, once we have encountered it. When on earth, Jesus, who is also the Lord of heaven by the way, made this starkly clear through a series of stories and warnings.

In the parable of Matthew 22:1-14, He likens the *'kingdom of the heavens'* (literal translation, meaning the whole spirit world we encounter after death, but Paradise in particular) to a feast given by a king (God the Father) for his son (Jesus). The feast is ready but the intended guests refuse to come. They even kill those sent to invite them. Angrily the king destroys *'those murderers'* and sends out invitations to the less worthy, *'both the bad and the good'*. Thus, the wedding hall is filled with motley guests, but then there's a problem. As the king enters to meet the guests, he sees a man who shouldn't be there because he has *'no wedding garment'*. Asked how he managed to get in without one, the man is *'speechless'*. Bound hand and foot he is ejected from the wedding feast and *'cast into outer darkness'*.

What, you might ask, is the *'wedding garment'* that evidently is the essential passport to entering bliss? In short, it is the *'robe of righteousness'* given to those who trust in Christ as their Saviour. It is what Paul described in Philippians 3:9 as *'...not my own righteousness which is from the law, but that which is through faith in Christ, the righteousness which is from God by faith'*.

You see, our attempts to make ourselves right with God by our own efforts fail miserably. Only the man Jesus has lived a holy life. He never sinned and throughout his life on earth did only that which was right and pleasing to God his Father. He died, rose to life again, and poured out his life-giving Spirit at Pentecost to make holy like Himself all those who put their trust in Him. But to be made holy, you must believe that He died for your sins, taking your rightful punishment in your place. When you do, you can be reconciled to God:

And you who were once enemies in your mind by wicked works, yet now He has reconciled in the body of his flesh through death (i.e., his crucifixion) to present you (to Himself) holy, and blameless, and above reproach in his sight.[118]

So, if Jesus' words count, then, while we may well enter the afterlife after death, we could find ourselves shut out from the Paradise that is part of it unless we wear the garment of righteousness that in Christ makes us acceptable to God. Already, we know from our own near-death experience, that we were sent back from the realm of bliss because we did not qualify to stay on.

Can we also be said to have *'climbed up some other way'*, that is other than through Jesus? In John 10:1-3 and 7, Jesus, speaking of the *'sheepfold'* (which I take to be heaven or Paradise) says that only He is the *'door of the sheep'*, i.e., the only way to heaven. And in verse one He gives a serious warning:

*Most assuredly, I say unto you he who does not enter the sheepfold by the **Door** (i.e., Himself), but climbs up some other way, the same is a thief and a robber. But He who enters by the door is the shepherd of the sheep. To Him the doorkeeper opens and the sheep hear his voice, and He calls out his own sheep by name and leads them out ... and the sheep follow Him for they know his voice. Yet they will by no means follow a stranger, but will flee from him, for they know not the voice of strangers.*

So, not only do we need a garment of righteousness to enter heaven in the afterlife, we also need, while still alive on earth, to

---

[118] Colossians 1:21-22

be called of Jesus, to hear His voice and to follow Him. This entails not listening to *'the voice of strangers'*, the spirits that would say it's ok to reject Jesus because you'll be let into heaven anyway. What's more, we need to ensure we have not climbed up to the sheepfold that is heaven *'some other way'*. For there are indeed spiritual *'thieves and robbers'* who would rob you of the right way to go to heaven, which, as said, is being made right with God through the death, burial and resurrection of Jesus Christ.

But there's more. We really do need to be saved. As the Apostle Peter told Israel's rulers, when warning them that the stone they had rejected (who is Jesus) had become the chief cornerstone …

> *Nor is there salvation in any other, for there is no other name under heaven given among men by which we must be saved.*[119]

To be saved we need to know that He has called each one of us by name; that He has called us to be with Him in Paradise, and that through Him we can have *'an inheritance in the saints of light'.*[120] A fuller excerpt of this passage reads:

> *Giving thanks unto the Father, who has* **qualified** *us to be partakers of the inheritance of the saints in the light. He has delivered us from the power of darkness and conveyed (or transferred) us into the kingdom of the Son of his love, in whom we have redemption through his blood, the forgiveness of sins (AMP).*

---

[119] Acts 4:12
[120] Colossians 1:12-13

So, the truth is that we need to be reconciled to God before we can go to be with Him in heaven. And that best needs to take place while we are still on earth and before our death. In fact, there is nothing to prevent us from being so reconciled, for God, for his part, has already reconciled the whole world, including us, to Himself.[121] All we have to do on our part is to have a change of heart (called repentance), turn toward Him, receive Him and be reconciled to Him.

Now, I hope you noticed the phrase *'saints of light'* in the above scripture. For it is those saints and the light they emanate that you likely saw in your near-death experience. And the inheritance spoken of is surely the right to stay on in their heavenly realm and not be sent back to the earthly body or, worse still, sent to some darker place.

---

[121] 2 Corinthians 5:18-19

Chapter 28 -
WHAT ON EARTH HAPPENS NEXT?

More importantly, what will God do next? For his intervention in the world, in our lives here below and in the future will make a huge difference. At present, we see our world stagger from one crisis to the next. Wars, plagues, earthquakes, floods, economic collapse and other disasters continue as they have for millennia. However, that will not always be the case. You see, at times, God steps into human history and drastically changes times, seasons and even the ages.

Right now, on God's big clock it's the age of grace. Peace, forgiveness and acceptance are freely lavished on all, whether Jew or Gentile or atheist, if they repent and turn to God. For nearly 2,000 years now, we've been living in this *dispensation of the grace of God'.* [122] It's been in force since Jesus told Paul that He (Jesus) had nailed the law, the one we couldn't keep, to his cross so we could be forgiven. [123]

But shortly, this age of being saved by God's gift of being *'saved by grace through faith alone'* [124] will end. God will then change the *'times and the seasons'* [125] bringing in a new and very different world that will be even better. And here's the thing.

---

[122] Ephesians 3:1-7
[123] Acts 2: 33, Colossians 2:14
[124] Ephesians 2:8
[125] Acts 1:7, 1 Thessalonians 5:1

That new and different world can be experienced now, ahead of time, by all who enter and get to stay on in the spirit realm that is variously called 'heaven' or 'Paradise', or the *world to come'.*[126]

For in the afterlife the only time is eternity. In other words, you can enter the future after death and enjoy all the blessings of the ages to come that God has promised without your waiting for the present age on earth to tick by.

And some such changes are stupendous. For example, the world to come Jesus and his Apostles spoke of, won't be harshly ruled by evil angels as the present world is. Hebrews 2:5 distinctly says, *'For He (God) has not put the world to come, of which we speak, in subjection to angels.'* Devils will no longer tempt and seduce mankind and the devil himself will be thrust through with the sword of God, his word.[127] Instead of evil spirits on high dictating the course of events,[128] the world will have a new ruler, the Lord Jesus Christ. For it is He who will *'bring forth judgement unto the Gentiles* (meaning all people).[129]

Those in heaven will live in and learn all the blessings of this world to come ahead of time before being resurrected back on earth in spiritual (i.e., not sinning) bodies to rule and reign with the Lord Jesus over earth and its people. Many Christians die, it seems, believing that the next event they will be aware of is the so-called 'Second Coming' of Christ. They expect to be resurrected to see the Lord come in fire and judgement to the earth. Indeed, as we have seen, Seventh Day Adventists believe they will simply sleep in the grave until the return of Jesus to earth.

---

[126] Matthew 12:32, Mark 10:30, Hebrews 2:5, 6:5
[127] Isaiah 24:21-22
[128] Ephesians 2:12
[129] Matthew 12:18

But what is to be made then of what Bible scholars term the 'intermediate state', by which they mean the interval of time between a person dying and them being resurrected to life again? Is a saved believer alive in some way in this time or asleep and dead? Now, it is true there will be a resurrection. Jesus promised that at the last day He would raise up those who put their trust in Him:

And this is the will of Him that sent Me; that everyone which seeth the Son, and believeth on Him, may have everlasting life, and I will raise him up at the last day. [130]

Jesus said unto her (Martha), I am the resurrection and the life: he who believes in Me, though he may die, he shall live. And whoever lives and believes in Me shall never die. [131]

However, it is what happens to us in the 'intermediate state' before our resurrection back to earth that is the main focus of this book as, indeed, it is also of the near-death experience. What's more, this interim life in the spirit realm is clearly what the Apostle Paul focussed on as he prepared to meet his own death. In Philippians 1:23 (AMP), he says:

My yearning desire is to depart (to be free of this world, to set forth) and to be with Christ, for that is far, far better.

In 2 Corinthians 5:1, Paul assures believers that if their earthly bodies are destroyed, they can have another body from God, *'a house not made with hands eternal in the heavens'*. And in verse 8-10 he says:

---

[130] John 6:40
[131] John 11:25-26

> *So, we are always confident knowing that while we are*
> *at home in the body (in our present earth life that is)*
> *we are absent from the Lord ... we are confident, yes,*
> *well pleased to be absent from the body and to be*
> *present with the Lord.*

The Amplified Bible makes the point more clearly:

> *[Yes] we have confident and hopeful courage and are*
> ***pleased*** *rather to be away from home **out of the body***
> *and be at home with the Lord. Therefore, whether we*
> *are at home [on earth away from Him] or away from*
> *home [and with Him] we are constantly ambitious and*
> *strive earnestly to be pleasing to Him. For we must all*
> *appear and be revealed as we are before the judgement*
> *seat of Christ, so that each one may receive [his pay]*
> *according to what he has done in the body, whether*
> *good or evil...*

Heaven then is the immediate and intermediate place the Lord wants us to call our home, or home away from home, if you will. Thus, in John 14:2 (AMP) He says:

> *In my Father's house there are many dwelling places*
> *(homes). If it were not so I would have told you, for I*
> *am going away to prepare a place for you ... I will*
> *come back again and take you to Myself that where I*
> *am you may be also.*

But beware. If the horror encountered by some NDErs is anything to go by, the *'many dwelling places'* in the afterlife include some neither you nor I would want to spend much time, still less eternity, in. Indeed, some experiencers report they were taken to the sort of hell where persons who rejected God, Christ and Bible truth in their life, now find themselves unable to cry for help to Him in the afterlife, again because they simply don't want to.

What is hell? My definition is that it is a dark place for those who throughout their earthly life rejected God and His offer of forgiveness and salvation through Jesus Christ. Accordingly, in the afterlife God respects their choice to have nothing to do with Him and thus after death they find themselves shut out from God and His heaven. Worse still, in this *'outer darkness'*[132] they do not repent or call on God to forgive them their sin because they do not see a need to do so. Thus, they are shut off from all the blessings God can give and remain immured in a Godless darkness they have created for themselves.

But even in this dire situation there may be hope. For God *'is not willing than any should perish but that all should come to repentance'.* [133] Is forgiveness and reconciliation still available in the afterlife, even for those who rejected the Saviour in the earthly life? I believe that it is. After all, didn't Christ after His resurrection preach the gospel to the dead and to the deceased who in the afterlife found themselves locked in a spiritual prison? Important verses penned by the Apostle Peter say that He did. Let's look at one passage in particular:

> *For Christ also suffered once for sins, the just for the unjust, that He might bring us to God, being put to death in the flesh but made alive by the Spirit **by whom He also went and preached to the spirits in prison,** who were formerly disobedient when once the Divine longsuffering waited in the days of Noah ...'* [134]

---

132 Matthew 8:12
133 2 Peter 3:9
134 1 Peter 3:18-19-20

The said spirits were not in prison during their life on earth but free to choose whether to board the ark and be saved with Noah or to reject the salvation offer he preached. Sadly, they did the latter. Accordingly, the only prison they could be held in when Jesus went to them is one in which they were held after death. It's an amazing testimony to the love of Christ that He would, thousands of years later visit them in Spirit to preach the gospel of salvation.

And it must have been salvation He preached, for surely, He did not go in the Spirit just to proclaim his own triumph over death and sin without sharing its benefits with them. In their life on earth, they rejected salvation with Noah aboard the ark. Now in the afterlife they are being given a second opportunity to repent and get right with God. For God is the God of *'the second time'*, or second chance, if you will.

This *'second time'* runs as a theme through Stephen's defence to the council and the high priest in Acts chapter six. Thus, just as Abraham was told to *'Get out of your country ... and come to a land I will show you'*, so over 400 years later the children of Israel enslaved in Egypt were also called out to go to the Promised Land, as it were 'the second time'. Moses was also given a second chance to be their deliverer when God appears to him in a burning bush, his first effort having ended in failure when he fled Egypt after killing an Egyptian. But it is Acts 6 verse 13, concerning Jacob's children resorting to Egypt to buy grain that says: *'And **the second time** Joseph was made known to his brothers...'* On their first visit they did not recognise Joseph as the brother they had sold into slavery but who was now master of Egypt's grain. But the second time they did.

In the same way, down through their history, Israel often failed to recognise their Saviour, God. So, Stephen asserts, He came to them as Messiah Jesus *'the second time'*. And even then, the leaders rejected Him because, as Stephen said:

> *You stiff-necked and uncircumcised in heart and ears.*
> *You do always resist the Holy Spirit; as your fathers*
> *did, so do you.*[135]

So, did the spirits of those who perished in Noah's time repent when the Lord visited them in their spiritual prison? We are not told plainly that is so but it is clearly inferred in 1 Peter 3:18-20:

> *For Christ also suffered once for sins, the just for the*
> *unjust, that He might bring us to God, being put to*
> *death in the flesh but made alive by the Spirit **by whom***
> ***He also went and preached to the spirits in prison,** who*
> *were formerly disobedient when once the Divine*
> *longsuffering waited in the days of Noah ...* ' [136]

Note that the subject here is Christ suffering *'the just for the unjust'*, not for the righteous, to bring them to God. The process of being saved is said to be that of being *'put to death in the flesh but made alive by the Spirit'*. The *'spirits in prison'* were put to death in the flesh when they died in the Flood. They could only be made *'alive by the Spirit'* by the Spirit of Jesus Christ visiting them in the afterlife. Did they repent and believe at his preaching to them in the afterlife? The clue is in verse 20 which says they were *'formerly disobedient'* clearly implying they were not so after Christ's preaching to them and therefore were obedient when He visited them.

---

[135] Acts 7:51
[136] 1 Peter 3:18-20

All of which means there can indeed be forgiveness upon repentance in the world after death. The fly in the ointment is that one must still repent. And, according to Jesus and the Bible, that can become impossible if one has received the gift of the Holy Spirit and then reneged and spat in His face as it were, as Hebrews 6:4-6 makes plain. For, it is impossible for those that *'fall away'* having *'tasted the heavenly gift and become partakers of the Holy Spirit and have tasted the good word of God and the powers of the age to come to renew themselves unto repentance'*.

God would freely forgive them if they did but turn to Him but because they will not repent, He cannot. That is why myriads of people are cut off from God and His blessings in the life to come. Yet for those who do repent, there is always a second chance, even in the afterlife. Thus, as we have seen, Jonah when dead repented, prayed to God and was saved. But it's far better to be saved while still alive on earth and thus be assured of being with God and being blessed by Him in the life to come.

In light of the after-death experience the Apostle Peter warns those who reject God in their earthly life that they will *'give an account to Him who is ready to judge the living and the dead'*. [137] He then goes on to say: *'For this reason the gospel was preached also to those who are **dead,** that they might be judged according to men in the flesh, but live according to God in the spirit'*. [138]

Thus, in preaching the gospel to the dead of the Old Testament period the Lord clearly was doing so for *'the second time'*. Is it possible the billions who have died in the last 2,000-plus years seemingly without accepting Christ as Saviour will also be given a second opportunity to be saved? I believe the

---

[137] 1 Peter 4:5
[138] 1 Peter 4:6

verses below offer this hope, especially if the specified timing is taken into account.

> *I then call on you in the sight of God and the Lord Jesus Christ who is **about** to judge the living and the **dead** according to his appearing and his kingdom (Interlinear Bible).*
>
> *I charge you therefore before God and the Lord Jesus Christ who **will** judge the living and the **dead** at his **appearing** and his **kingdom** (KJV).* [139]
>
> *And He [Jesus] charged us [his appointed apostles] to preach to the people and to bear solemn testimony that He is the God-appointed and God-ordained Judge of the living and of the **dead** (AMP).* [140]

In his *'Greek-English Interlinear Bible'*, Jay Green brings out an important truth in 2 Timothy 4:1. It is that in the Apostle Paul's lifetime, the Lord was **'about to'** judge the living and the dead. It is an imminent event that has yet to take place. When will He do so? Clearly from 2 Timothy 4:1 when he brings in his **kingdom** at his **appearing**.

To define the terms: the **kingdom** is when God fully enforces his heavenly rule on earth – the Lord's Prayer says, *'Your kingdom come, your will be done on earth as it is in heaven'*. And his **appearing** (*epiphanea*, which means a powerful shining forth of his glory) must be seen as a separate event in which He takes up his office of King of heaven on earth.

---

[139] 2 Timothy 4:1
[140] Acts 10:42

Question: Has the Lord **appeared** yet? No. Has He brought in his **kingdom** on earth yet? No. Has He started judging the living and the dead yet? No. But He will very shortly. That is why Paul urges us to be:

> *Awaiting and looking for (the fulfilment, the realisation of our) blessed hope, even the glorious appearing of our great God and Saviour Christ Jesus (the Messiah, the Anointed One) (AMP).* [141]

The truth is that while both Old Testament saints and deceased New Testament believers enjoy rest with Jesus in heaven now, the bulk of humanity does not. And while the imprisoned spirits of those who disobeyed in Noah's time have had the gospel preached to them, it would seem the remaining dead have not.

But, Paul assures us, when Christ appears in glory (Titus 2:13, 2 Timothy 4:1) they will be so addressed.

---

[141] Titus 2:13

Chapter 29 -
A TALE OF TWO BODIES

There's the exciting novel of the French Revolution, *'A Tale of Two Cities'* and the quite different 'Tale of Two Bodies', which, apparently, is a feature of the life to come. Fact is, there's so much more to the afterlife experience than we can dream of.

For example, would you like a body that can never sin and can pass through walls? Well, in the realm beyond it seems you can have one. And, believe it or not, some out-of-the-body experiencers say it was not just in their spirit but also in a new and spiritual body that they experienced heaven. Of course, the new body is left behind when they return to their earthly bodies. So, the transformation is only temporary.

Choo Thomas, for example, in her book *'Heaven is so Real'*[142] says that seventeen times she was taken on visits to heaven by Jesus and was given not only a crown and white robe to wear on each occasion but also a new body which was young, vibrant and beautiful – a recapturing of her teenage vigour, if you will.

Her new, heavenly body, she believes, was a foretaste of the forever spiritual body she will have after death when she reaches heaven. What's more, during her trips to the Beyond, there was physical contact with Jesus Himself through her new body, she

---

[142] *Heaven is so Real* by Choo Thomas, published by Charisma House, Strang Book Group, Florida 2003, 2006.

avers. The Lord took her hand to lead on a guided tour of heaven and even gave her a hug.

It seems such new bodies will not grow old, their faces will never wrinkle, their teeth will remain white and even and the posture will stay straight. Bodily handicaps from earthly life will vanish, hair will never grey and 'the radiance of youth will glow from our eyes', Choo asserts.

Her afterlife metamorphosis of bodily form poses the question of just when believers at large should expect to get their new bodies. Will they have to wait until the resurrection Jesus promised would take place 'at the last day'? Will new bodies only be given out at the so-called rapture? Or will our new bodies be given us on entry into heaven? Going further, we might ask if all who enter the afterlife receive new bodies what will they be like?

I don't know the full answer to these questions but from a limited Bible study I make the following observations and suggestions:

First up, there is no mention of people getting new bodies in the Bible account of the so-called 'rapture', neither is that word itself ever used in scripture. What is prophesied in 1 Thessalonians 4:15-18, however, is a resurrection from the dead at the *coming of the Lord'*. Firstly, of those *'who sleep in Jesus'*. Thus, we are told by Paul that the *'dead in Christ will rise first, then we who are alive shall be caught up together with them in the clouds to meet the Lord in the air. Thus, we shall ever be with the Lord'*.

Please note, there is no mention here in this passage of anyone getting new bodies. Neither are new, spiritual bodies mentioned in Romans 14:10 where we are told, *'... we shall stand before the judgement seat of Christ'*. And here *'all'* does indeed mean all; you, me and everybody else, for *'we must all appear before the judgement seat of Christ'*.

This judgement occurs in a special day earmarked by the Apostle Paul as one in which *'God will judge the secrets of men by Jesus Christ according to my gospel'*.[143] That day is in fact the *'day of Christ'* referred to seven times in Paul's epistles in the KJV. If correctly treated as separate from other days such as the 'day of man'[144] and the *'day of the Lord'*[145] it is the day when *'...the Lord Jesus Christ ... will judge the living and the dead at his appearing and his kingdom'*.

There is no mention of new bodies in these scriptures but there is in 2 Corinthians chapter five. Here in verse 1, we are told **when** we believers will receive our wonderful new and very spiritual body. In short, it is when our present body, *'...our earthly house, this tent, is destroyed'* and, by implication, we have died and find ourselves in heaven.

Now isn't a new body like that something to really look forward to?

---

[143] Romans 2:16
[144] Luke 22:53, 1 Corinthians 4:3
[145] 1 Thessalonians 5:2, Joel 2:1.

BIBLIOGRAPHY

Berman, Philip L., The Journey Home, Simon & Schuster Trade, 1996.

Brubaker, Don, Absent from the Body, Peninsula Publishing, 1995.

Eby, Richard, Caught up into Paradise, Baker Books, 1984.

Fenimore, Angie, Beyond the Darkness, Bantam Books Inc., 1996.

Moody, Jr., Raymond A., The Last Laugh, Hampton Roads Publishing Co. Inc., 1999.

Williams, Kevin R., Nothing Better Than Death, 2002, Xlibris Corporation, USA.

Melvin, Bryan W., A Land Unknown: Hell's Dominion, Xulon Press, 2005

About the Author

The author John Dudley Aldworth has a prophetic teaching ministry and a passion for seeing and experiencing more of God. He holds that a manifestation of the Lord's personal anointing, bringing comfort, healing and deliverance, will be experienced whenever and wherever the word of the imminent Day of Christ is believed.

John has had a wide and varied career in journalism. A former sub-editor on Britain's Daily Mail, in New Zealand, he has variously edited The Accountant's Journal, The New Zealand Journal of Agriculture and the New Zealand Gardener. A former business editor of the Waikato Times, he has also worked for Wellington's Evening Post, The Dominion and Hamilton This Week.

The following books are all available online at any bookstore, can be borrowed from your local library or, if in New Zealand, you can purchase direct from the author: john.aldworth@hotmail.com

OTHER BOOKS BY JOHN DUDLEY ALDWORTH

Forbidden History (2016) 978-0-473-35264-6

Did Phoenician and Chinese mariners populate New Zealand 2,000 years ago?
Were Mediterranean voyagers the first Polynesians?
Did ancient Celts flee war in the Middle East, sail to New Zealand and form a nation that lived in peace for over 1,000 years?

This book views New Zealand History through the Paatupaiarehe and Waitaha traditions rather than the perspective of Maori and latter-day European accounts. In support, it cites rock-solid artifacts, important world historical research, and the undeniable discovery of old shipwrecks that brough pre-Maori people to this 'Far Away Land'.

Noah's Land (2019) 978-0-473-49172-7

Did the great Patriarch colonise New Zealand in 2,225BC?

The cover of the book features a photograph of the author beside a statue found at Purekireki Marae, Pirongia, which depicts an ancestor of the Paatupaiarehe people and Nuku (Noah in the ancient language of New Zealand) who is said to be their founding father.

So, was Noah the first to find and settle this country? This book goes on a search for the answers.

The Glory of His Day (2022) 978-0-473-62478-1

WHAT WILL GOD'S TOMORROW BE LIKE?

A new age is about to dawn. Will it see God wreak his wrath on the world or bring in a wonderful tomorrow? The answer may lie in a Bible phrase ignored and forgotten today. Yet, in the early church the 'day of Christ', mentioned seven times in Paul's epistles, was the apostles' 'blessed hope'.

Saints eagerly looked for Christ to appear in a blaze of piercing light to curb evil, reward saints, banish sickness and poverty and save the world. To the author the nearness of this glorious day, Christ's own day, is the vital truth God would impress upon believers at this time.

He is convinced the now imminent 'appearing' will be when the Lord is revealed in all his glory for all the world to see and the time for Him to bring in a whole new and blessed day in man's experience.